Flames of Wisdom

Spiritual Teachings for Daily Life

by

David Beck

© 2016 Theosis Books

ISBN: 978-1540373731
Printed in the United States of America.

You have stretched out the heavens like a tent,

You have laid the beams of Your chambers on the waters,

You make the clouds Your chariot,

You ride on the wings of the wind,

You make Your angels winds;

And Your servants flames of fire.

Ps. 104:3-4

- from the translation found in *A Manual of the Hours of the Orthodox Church*, compiled by Archimandrite Cherubim; Monastery of the Paraclete, Attica, Greece.

Abba Lot went to see Abba Joseph and said to him, "Abba, as far as I can, I say my little office, I fast a little, I pray and meditate, I live in peace as far as I can, I purify my thoughts What else can I do?" Then the old man stood up and stretched his hands toward heaven. His fingers became like ten lamps of fire and he said to him, "If you will, you can become all flame."

- from *The Sayings of the Desert Fathers: The Alphabetical Collection*

3

Acknowledgments

Much has changed since this was originally published, in 1994. Two of the mentors I acknowledged have left this world: Dr. Charles Ashanin and Fr. Nathaniel Eichner. May their memory be eternal! They along with Brian McDonald and Fr. John Schmidt served as guides for my entrance into the Church.

Thanks to Marty Nagy whose friendship has inspired many great conversations that shaped my approach not just to writing, but to life in general. I am grateful as well for the love and support from Fr. David Wey, our former priest Hieromonk Joseph (Morris) and the community of Sts. Constantine and Elena Orthodox Church of which I am a member.

Thank you to Theodore Nottingham for his willingness to put *Flames of Wisdom* back in print through Theosis Books.

Last and certainly not least, I am grateful for the love and encouragement I undeservedly receive from Susie, my wife, and my son, Michael and my daughter, Christina.

Flames of Wisdom

Table of Contents

Flames of Wisdom

Introduction

With great pains one must seek out an undeceived instructor, and if we do not find one, then the holy fathers have commanded us to take instruction from the Divine Scripture and the teachings of the Holy Fathers.

-St. Nilus of Sora

Living in this post-Christian-age, Christians find it increasingly difficult to maintain a burning fire for their faith. We are surrounded by a culture that not only disregards Christian beliefs, but has made it illegal for any religious display that might offend those of another faith or of no faith at all. Our culture—its music, art, and entertainment—is not only iconoclastic but anti-iconic. The creation that glorifies and speaks of its Creator has been replaced largely with ugly concrete monuments that speak only of mankind's condition without God.

In such a culture it should be no surprise to find few God-bearing spiritual fathers and mothers. In ancient times, even as recent as nineteenth-century Russia, Christians would seek the counsel and advice of holy men and women, most of whom spent their lives in monasteries and secluded places. These holy people not only gave godly advice but often performed great miracles. They were a light in the world, a city on a hill that could not be hidden. While we can take comfort in their intercessions, we can no longer go on pilgrimages to seek their spiritual wisdom. Some holy elders still exist here and there, hidden in different places around the world, but their inaccessibility makes it difficult for the lay person to discover their wisdom and counsel. Yet, if the Fathers of the Church needed spiritual guidance, how much more do we, in this age of comfortable materialism, secular humanism, and spiritual impoverishment, need the wisdom of a spiritual director?

Each of us needs spiritual guidance. It is important that we pray for a spiritual elder. Many find such guidance from their parish priests; others live close enough to monasteries, that they can receive instruction from monks or nuns. One might find a layperson who is devout and has experienced enough in the Christian life that godly counsel might be received from him or her. I.M. Kontzevitch writes, "Only a man who successfully traversed the path of spiritual labor himself can lead other along this path." Regardless, we must pray that God will send us that person to whom we can express our inner-most needs and struggles and whose wisdom and advice will better equip us to fight the good fight. Today such a person is rare and not easily found. This problem does not affect only the layperson. Even some monastics have lived in times and places where spiritual eldership was lacking. Regarding this problem within monasticism, Kontzevitch writes,

> If a contemporary ascetic can no longer find an experienced spiritual

11

director, through no fault of his own
but by reason of a complete absence
of the latter, he nevertheless should
not lose heart and leave his ascetic
endeavor. According to the advice
of St. Nilus of Sora, a monk of today
must turn to the Scriptures and the
writings of the holy Fathers; he must
not be alone in this, but seek the
counsel of the more proficient
brethren though at the same time
comparing their counsel with
Scripture.

Thus the answer for the monastic and the
layperson is twofold: First, one must read and
meditate on the words of Scripture and the
counsels and teachings of the Holy Fathers.
Second, this reading must not be done alone. It has
to take place in the context of the Church. As
members of the Body we will find the
encouragement as well as the proper direction
needed to walk in the fullness of the faith. Holy
Scripture should direct our lives; however, we need
assistance knowing how to apply the guidance and
medicine to our lives. We need guides, guides who

will instruct according to the tradition of the Church, as given to us by the Holy Spirit.

John Cassian (circa 365-435) warns us about relying on our own judgment. He states:

> We will most easily come to a precise knowledge of true discernment if we follow the paths of our elders, if we do nothing novel, and if we do not presume to decide anything on the basis of our own private judgment. Instead let us in all things travel the road laid down for use by the tradition of our elders and by the goodness of their lives.

This idea of relying not on our own judgment goes against our Western heritage and its emphasis on individualism. Yet Cassian was adamant concerning this point:

> All the skills and disciplines devised by human talent for the benefit of this temporal life can be laid hold of, observed, understood, but only with the necessary help of an instructor. Now the spiritual life is unseen and hidden, open only the purest heart. Here the fact of going wrong brings harm that is not of this world and cannot easily be rectified. Rather, it causes the loss

of the soul and everlasting death. So then how stupid it is to believe that only this way of life has no need of a teacher.

In other words, the need for instruction in the spiritual matters is great. In our modern era, more and more emphasis is placed on education. Without college degrees or vocational training, it is increasingly difficult to find a job. If instruction is needed to find a job, how much more do we need instruction in the spiritual life, where our very souls are at stake?

We must rely therefore on those God-bearing elders who lived and taught in the Church tradition. Without such teachers we must immerse ourselves in the writings of our Holy Fathers. Kontzevitch's statement concerning the need to read the writings of holy teachers for guidance is corroborated by the saints themselves. St. Seraphim of Sarov gives the same advice:

> But if one cannot find an instructor able to direct one into the contemplative life, in this case one must be directed by Holy

Scripture... Likewise one must endeavor to read through the writings of the of the Fathers, and strive as much as possible, according to one's strength, to fulfill what they teach, and in this fashion, little by little ascend from the active life to the perfection of contemplation.

St. John Climacus warns, "Those who rely on themselves and think they have no need of any guide are deceiving themselves."

Fr. Seraphim Rose saw these writings as a gift from God, a gift that is invaluable in an age deficient of spiritual elders. He writes,

These writings of the Holy Fathers, even those dealing with the highest form of spiritual life, have been preserved *for us*, so that even, when it might seem that there are not God-bearing elders left at all, we may still have the unerring words of the Holy Fathers to guide us in leading a God-pleasing and zealous life.

Similarly, St. Ignatius Brianchaninov states, "Because of the diminishing of Spirit-bearing instructors, the reading of the Fathers' writings has become the main guide for those who wish to be saved and even attain Christian perfection."

This book presents the teachings and counsels of several saints and Fathers of the Church. Their brief summaries will deal mostly with one, maybe two, issues relevant to the Christians in the modern world. These chapters are not abstract theological treatises. I have attempted to glean from them the most practical aspects of their writings. In short, what follows is the God-inspired counsel of godly men who, through their words and supplications, can lead us to a closer walk with our God, kindling within our hearts and minds their flames of wisdom.

I

St. Seraphim of Sarov

On the Acquisition of the Holy Spirit

Having purified the soul beforehand by repentance and good deeds, and with faith in the Crucified, having closed the bodily eyes, immerse the mind within the heart, in which place cry out with the invocation of our Lord Jesus Christ; and then, to the measure of one's zeal and warmth of spirit toward the Beloved, a man finds in the invoked name a delight which awakens the desire to seek higher illumination.

-St. Seraphim of Sarov

Perhaps the best-known Orthodox saint of modern times is St. Seraphim of Sarov. He is known in the Orthodox and non-Orthodox world alike. Being a charismatic figure, this Russian saint is often misunderstood as an independent man who had great spiritual experiences outside the Church. This misunderstanding is perpetuated often by those who teach a type of spirituality that is not in accordance with the Church. St. Seraphim never left the Church and was always under Her direction and authority.

St. Seraphim was born in 1759. At the age of nineteen, he left his boyhood home of Kursk, to make a pilgrimage to Kiev. On his journey he was instructed by a recluse to go to Sarov. Shortly afterwards, he went to the monastery there, where he spent the rest of his life.

In 1804 he received permission from the Abbot to become a hermit. Living in the forest, his only contact with people was on Sunday, when he returned to the monastery to attend the Liturgy and receive Holy Communion. In 1806 St. Seraphim was attacked and beaten severely by a band of robbers. During a time of healing, he was blessed with a vision of the Blessed Virgin Mary. As a result of the beating, however, St. Seraphim was lame, forced to use a staff while walking. (This "deformity" is usually depicted on the icons of St. Seraphim. He is often seen bent over, leaning on his staff.)

By request of the monastery elders, he returned to his cell in 1810. There he continued his silence and seclusion. He read one Gospel each day and read the entire New Testament each week. While in his cell he had many visions of the saints and one time saw the mansions of heaven. After five years of seclusion in his cell, St. Seraphim began receiving visitors. Later he returned to the forest where he received thousands of pilgrims, granting spiritual counsel to all. His gifts of healing, clairvoyance, and wisdom were known throughout Russia. He died on January 2, 1833, while kneeling before an icon of the Mother of God of "Tender Feeling." He was canonized in 1903.

Although he never put his teachings into writing, his words of instruction were recorded by those who knew him. His teaching on the acquisition of the Holy Spirit is taken from a conversation with

N. A. Motovilov. Motovilov's manuscript was found in 1902, lying in a trash pile, in an attic. The Introduction to the *Little Russian Philokalia*, Volume 1, states that his instructions "contain no new teaching, but simply repeat in modern times the age-old Christian teaching of the great Fathers whom he constantly cites: Sts. Basil the Great, Gregory the Theologian, John Chrysostom, Macarius the Great, Dionysius the Areopagite, Ambrose of Milan, Isaac the Syrian, Simeon the New Theologian, the Fathers of the *Philokalia*."

Motovilov tells us that he came upon St. Seraphim on a gloomy day that saw eight inches of snow on the ground with more falling. The great saint sat on a tree stump opposite Motovilov. He began teaching Motovilov of the true aim of the Christian life:

> Prayer, fasting, vigil and all other Christian practices, however good they may be in themselves, do not constitute the aim of our Christian life, although they serve as an

indispensable means of reaching this end. The true aim of our Christian life consists in the acquisition of the Holy Spirit. As for fasts, and vigils, and prayer, and almsgiving, and every good deed done for Christ's sake, they are only means of acquiring the Holy Spirit of God.

From here, St. Seraphim explains how we acquire the Holy Spirit.

First, we must not confuse this "acquisition" with the initial receiving of the Holy Spirit during baptism and chrismation. St. Seraphim states that the "fire-infusing grace of the Holy Spirit which was given to us all, the faithful of Christ, in the Sacrament of Holy Baptism, is sealed by the Sacrament of Chrismation on the chief parts of our body as appointed by the Holy Church, the eternal keeper of this grace." What St. Seraphim emphasizes, however, is the daily acquisition of His presence.

When asked how to receive the Holy Spirit, St. Seraphim says that "prayer gives us [the Holy Spirit] most of all, for [prayer] is always at hand, so to speak, as an instrument for acquiring the grace of the Holy

Spirit." The reason prayer is such an important tool is that opportunity for prayer is never lacking: "Prayer is always possible for everyone, rich and poor, noble and humble, strong and weak, healthy and sick, righteous and sinful."

An interesting aspect to St. Seraphim's teaching on prayer is that he insists that we pray only until the Holy Spirit visits us. He tells us that

> we must pray only until God the Holy Spirit descends on us in measures of His heavenly grace known to Him. And when he deigns to visit us, we must stop praying. Why should we then pray to Him, "Come and abide in us and cleanse us from all impurity and save our souls, O God (sic) One," when he has already come to us to save us who trust in Him, and truly call on His holy name, that humbly we may receive Him, the Comforter in the mansions of our souls hungering and thirsting for His coming?

After the Holy Spirit descends upon us, not only must we cease praying, but we should remain still. He states that to "be still" (Ps. 46:10) does not only mean we are to be still to "worldly affairs." When the Holy Spirit visits us we must be dead not only to the cares of this must world, but we must be dead to prayer, too:

> The soul speaks and converses during prayer, but at the descent of the Holy Spirit we must remain in complete silence, in order to hear clearly and intelligibly all the words of eternal life which He will then deign to communicate. Complete soberness of soul and spirit, and chaste purity of body is required at the same time.

While St. Seraphim emphasizes the importance of prayer, he does not, by any means, make it the sole means of acquiring the Holy Spirit. He teaches us that we must use whatever works best: "if prayer and watching gives you more of God's grace, watch and pray; if fasting gives you much of the spirit of God, fast; if almsgiving gives you more, give alms. Weigh every virtue done for Christ's sake in this manner." If, however, we are not receiving the Holy Spirit, "we must discover why and for what reason our Lord God the Holy Spirit has willed to abandon us; we must seek Him again through His goodness."

Toward the end of their conversation, Motovilov, perplexed and confused, asks the wise saint how is he to know he has received the Holy Spirit. St. Seraphim replies,

> But there is nothing incomprehensible here. This failure to understand has come about because we have departed from the simplicity of the original Christian knowledge. Under the pretext of education, we have reached such darkness of ignorance that what the ancients understood so clearly seems to us incomprehensible.

He goes on to tell Motovilov that enlightenment is a sign of the acquisition of the Holy Spirit:

> I will tell you something else, so that you may understand still more clearly what is meant by the grace of God, how to recognize it and how its action is manifested particularly in those who are enlightened by it. The grace of the Holy Spirit is light which enlightens men. In other words, the grace of the Holy Spirit which is expressed in the Law by the words of the Lord's commandments is my lamp and light. And if this grace of the Holy Spirit. . .did not enlighten me amidst the darkness of the cares which are

inseparable from the high calling of my royal rank, whence should I get a spark of light to illumine my way on the path of life which is darkened by the ill-will of my enemies?

If this reply seems somewhat cryptic, if not vague, one must remember what St. Seraphim is attempting to describe: a spiritual state which is beyond words and concepts. Yet what he is describing is not solely for the ascetic or mystic, but for all Christians. Who can describe the joy, the peace, the "inner voice" of the Holy Spirit with mere words? Thus St. Seraphim is equating the acquisition of the Holy Spirit with the ability to know and discern the commandments of God: not just an intellectual understanding, but an inner enlightenment within the heart of the believer.

Much of what St. Seraphim tells Motovilov is ambiguous. Motovilov himself is trying constantly to "pin down" an answer from the saint. Yet what is being described can only be experienced, not verbalized.

Perhaps sensing the inadequacy of his words, St. Seraphim took Motovilov by the shoulders and said, "We are both in the Spirit of God now, my son. Why don't you look at me?"

Motovilov replied, "I cannot look, Father, because your eyes are flashing like lightning. Your face has become brighter than the sun, and my eyes ache with pain."

But St. Seraphim tells him not to be alarmed for "you yourself have become as bright as I am." He then says to Motovilov that he, St. Seraphim, had prayed silently to the Lord that God would reveal to Motovilov's eyes the descent of the Holy Spirit.

He describes what he saw on the face of St. Seraphim:

> After these words I glanced at his face and there came over me an even greater awe. Imagine in the centre of the sun, in the dazzling light of its midday rays, the face of a man talking to you. You see the movement of his lips and the changing expression of his eyes, you hear his voice, you feel someone holding your shoulders; yet you do not see his hands, you do not even see yourself or his figure, but only a blinding light spreading far around for

several yards and illumining with its glaring sheen both the snow-blanket which covered the forest glade and the snow-flakes which besprinkled me and the great elder.

Then the saint asked him how he felt. Motovilov said that he felt a great peace and calmness, an extraordinary sweetness and joy.

St. Seraphim replies, "When the Spirit of God comes down to man and overshadows him with the fulness of His inspiration, then the human soul overflows with unspeakable joy, for the Spirit of God fills with joy whatever He touches." He concludes by saying,

> Yet however comforting may be this joy which you now feel in your heart, it is nothing in comparison with that of which the Lord Himself by the mouth of His apostle said that that joy **eye had not seen nor ear heard, nor has it entered into the heart of man what God has prepared for them that love Him** (I Cor. 2:9). Foretastes of that joy are given to us now, and if they fill our souls with such sweetness,

well-being and happiness, what shall
we say of that joy which has been
prepared in heaven for those who
weep here on earth?

With St. Seraphim of Sarov we find no systematic
theology. Moreover, we have no words written by his
own hand. Yet his conversation with Motovilov on the
acquisition of the Holy Spirit survives and is perhaps
his best-known teaching. But like many of the saints,
his life is his teaching.

For better or for worse St. Seraphim is more
widely known for his spiritual experiences than for his
theology. What teachings we do have, recorded by
others, are in accord with the early Fathers and with
that of the Church.

What makes St. Seraphim's teaching on the
acquisition of the Holy Spirit seem somewhat cryptic
and ambiguous is two-fold: First, he interchanges the
term "receiving the Holy Spirit" with "receiving God's
grace." At the same time, he seems to make a
distinction between the acquisition of the Holy Spirit
during baptism and chrismation and the acquisition in

the daily walk of the believer. Second, as mentioned earlier, he attempts to explain the unexplainable. When reading this account, one senses Motovilov's frustration as he tries to gain a clear criteria or some formula that will let him know when he receives the Holy Spirit in his daily life. Only through a miracle does he begin to understand.

While we may never experience such an illumination of the Holy Spirit as they did, we can learn from this account. First, the aim of our life should be to receive the Holy Spirit each day. According to St. Seraphim, prayer is the best way, yet certainly not the only way. When we sense the Holy Spirit has descended upon us, we should be still and listen to what He might say to us. Signs of the Holy Spirit's descent on the believer are peace, sweetness and joy. If we do not sense these fruits in our lives, we must ask the Lord why and then pray for His mercy.

Pray for us, St. Seraphim, that we too may acquire the grace of the Holy Spirit.

Bibliography

Motovilov, M. A. "The Acquisition of the Holy
Spirit," from *Little Russian Philokalia,
Vol. 1: St. Seraphim.* Platina, CA: St.
Herman of Alaska Brotherhood,
1978. (71-96).

II

St. Silouan

On Knowing God

Blessed is the soul that knows her Creator and has grown to love Him, for she has found perfect rest in Him.

- St. Silouan

St. Silouan is one of those rare men of the twentieth century who embodied the teachings of the early fathers and saints. He was born in 1866 in a small village in Russia. His name "in this world" was Symeon Ivanovich Antonov. Before his conversion Symeon joined an *artel,* a group of young artists who lived and worked together. Like many young men

Symeon led a life of dissipation, drinking, and carousing with his friends.

One day, during a celebration of the village patron saint, Symeon was approached by a young drunken cobbler who, wanting to impress the local girls, began picking a fight with him. Symeon was a strong young man of average height and of stocky build. Fearing that the girls would laugh at him if he turned his back, he threw a powerful punch to the chest of the young cobbler. The man stumbled back, blood trickling from his mouth. Then he turned on the cobbler's brother, asking if he wanted what his brother had just received. The young man ran away while his brother still lay unconscious on the ground. Symeon, as well as the other villagers, thought the man was dead. Finally, with help, the young man was able to rise and make it home.

Shortly after this incident Symeon had a strange dream. In this dream he saw a snake slithering into his mouth and crawling down his throat. He awoke immediately, repulsed at what he had seen. Then he heard an unusually beautiful voice saying, "Just as you found it loathsome to swallow a snake in your dream, so I find your ways ugly to look upon." Although he saw no one, Symeon was convinced that the sweet, gentle voice he heard was that of the Blessed Virgin. This incident changed his life.[1]

Symeon began repenting of his old ways and desired nothing else than to enter a monastery. In 1892 he traveled to the Holy Mountain, Mount Athos in Northern Greece. There he became a monk and received the name Silouan. He spent the rest of his life there, fighting the good fight and helping others do the same. He acquired the title "staretz," a Russian term for "elder." A staretz is, in short, a spiritual guide and director. After forty-six years of the monastic life, St. Silouan died peacefully, in 1938. In 1987, he was canonized.

For St. Silouan, knowing God should be the goal of all people everywhere. No greater achievement is there than to know one's Creator, and this knowledge penetrates the whole person, not just the mind or heart: "The Lord is made known in the Holy Spirit, and the Holy Spirit pervades the *entire* man— soul, mind and body." And it is only by the Holy Spirit that we can truly know Him. In the Holy Spirit, not only can we know God, but we can also become aware of the "great cloud of witnesses" that surrounds us (Heb. 12:1). He writes that "the Creator Himself of heaven and earth and every created thing gives us to know Him in the Holy Spirit. In this same Holy Spirit we know the Mother of God, the Angels and Saints, and our spirit burns with love for them."

When our knowledge of God increases, our desire for earthly pleasures decreases: "We live a long time on this earth and we love the beauty of the earth: the sky and the sun, gardens, sea and river, forest and meadow, music too, and all the beauties of the world. But when the soul comes to know our Lord Jesus Christ then she has no further desire for the things of the earth." He also states, "The spirit of the man who has come to know God by the Holy Spirit burns day and night with the love of God, and his soul can form no earthly attachment."

St. Silouan also taught that it is one thing to believe in God but quite another to know Him: "Enlightened by Baptism, people believe in God; but there are some who even know Him. To believe in God is good, but it is more blessed to know God." He makes this distinction again when he writes, "There is nothing more precious than to know God; and nothing worse than not to know Him. But he too is blessed who, though he does not know, yet believes." Thus it is good and noble to believe in God, but it is the greatest achievement of all human beings to know God.

How is it then that we come to know God? St. Silouan warns us that the knowledge of God comes not from books but from obedience: "We may study as much as we will but we shall still not come to know the Lord unless we live according to His commandments, for the Lord is not made known through learning but by the Holy Spirit." We see therefore that we can come to know God through obeying His commands and by the Holy Spirit.

In what way must we be obedient? For St. Silouan, the answer is two-fold: through humility and by loving our enemies. We can infer from his writings that obedience to Christ is summed up in these two virtues. Moreover, humility is central to the Christian life. We cannot love our enemies, much less know God, without a humble spirit.

To know God, to come to a deep knowledge of Him, takes no certain amount of intellectual gifting and is certainly not dependent on one's status in the community or one's position in the Church. In fact, St. Silouan writes, "The poorest wretch may humble himself and know God in the Holy Spirit. There is no need of possessions to know God, only of humility." It is reassuring to know that we can come to God as we are, with humble hearts and minds, and not only approach God but increasingly come to know Him more deeply.

St. Silouan teaches us that knowing God is the greatest achievement of all creation. And if we can know Him through humility, then humility is what we must strive for. He writes,

> To learn Christ-like humility is a great good. Only to the humble does the Lord reveal Himself in the Holy Spirit, but if we do not humble ourselves we shall not see God. Humility is the light in which we may behold the light which is God, as the Psalmist sang: 'In Thy light we shall see light.'

This godly elder teaches us that we should pray for humility, that we may live obediently and increase our knowledge of God. Here is an example of St. Silouan's prayer for humility:

> O God of Mercy, Thou knowest our infirmity. I beseech Thee, grant me a humble spirit, for in Thy mercy Thou dost enable the humble soul to live according to

41

Thy will. Thou dost reveal Thy
mysteries to her. Thou givest her
to know Thee and the infinity of
Thy love for us.

This prayer is a good one for each of us to pray. It exemplifies St. Silouan's belief that humility precedes our knowing God.

As we increase in humility, so too will our knowledge of God increase, which in turn serves to instill even more humility, and consequently a deeper knowledge of God. He writes that "when the soul comes to know the Lord in the Holy Spirit, how humble and meek He is, she sees herself as the worst of all sinners and is happy to sit in shabby raiment among the ashes like Job, beholding other men in the Holy Spirit shining in the likeness of Christ." Thus humility is the key to knowing God, and our knowledge of Him increases as we see ourselves in His light and become increasingly humble.

Second, the elder teaches us that, through our love for our enemies, we come to know God. He writes that "the man who thinks with malice of his enemies has not God's love within him and does not know God; for God is love." These words echo the same idea that is be found in John's first epistle: "He who does not love does not know God; for God is love (I John 4:8). The staretz also states that "he who will not love his enemies cannot come to know the Lord and the sweetness of the Holy Spirit." He then affirms these statements by writing, "The man who loves his enemies soon comes to know the Lord in the Holy Spirit."

> Not only must we love our enemies, but we must also pray for them: It is a great thing in the sight of God to pray for those who hurt our feelings and injure us. For this the Lord will grant us grace, and by the Holy Spirit we shall come to know the Lord, and then we shall bear every affliction with joy for His sake, and the Lord will give us love for the whole world. We shall ardently desire the good of all men, and pray for all as for our own souls.

Loving and praying for our enemies not only allows us to know God in a deeper way, but it increases our love and empathy toward those who injure us.

Some may wonder if they have actual "enemies." While we may not have outward persecution as some Christians have had to bear, we still have others who, by their words or attitudes, wound us and cause bitter feelings to grow within us. Thus when we are treated rudely by someone we do not even know; or when someone infringes upon our "rights"; we must not only bear these remarks and actions, but we must pray for those who treat us badly, even if it is just a quick prayer for the person who pulled out recklessly in front of us while driving. It is in these small ways, that we prepare our souls for greater trials and persecutions. At the same time, as the elder teaches us, our love for others, for the whole world, will increase. And with that increasing love, so too will our knowledge of God increase. He writes, "There is love in small degrees, medium love and perfect love; and the more perfect our love the more perfect our knowledge."

To know God, therefore, St. Silouan teaches us that humility and love for our enemies are

44

necessary. In fact, the elder sees humility as the beginning of the Christian life. Without a humble spirit, we cannot hope to love our enemies or anyone else in a truly Christian way. Yet the struggle to know God through these virtues is a lifelong one. St. Silouan encourages us with these words: "Thus the soul spends her whole life waging war. But do not lose heart over the struggle, for the Lord loves a brave fighter."

Pray for us, St. Silouan, that through increasing humility and love for our enemies, we may come to know God.

Notes

1. This incident is recorded in Archimandrite's biography of Staretz Silouan, *The Monk of Mount Athos* (10-12). Translated from the Russian by Rosemary Edmonds. Crestwood, New York: St. Vladimir's Press, 1975. This book gives an account of the elder's life as well as a summary of his teachings.

Bibliography

Archimandrive Sophrony. Wisdom from Mount Athos: *The Writings of Staretz Silouan Wisdom from Mount Athos: The Writings of Staretz Silouan 1866-1938*. Translated from the Russian by Rosemary Edmonds. Crestwood, New York: St. Vladimir's Seminary Press, 1974.

III

St. Theophan the Recluse

On Communion with God

The basic principle is that communion
with God is the beginning, middle and
end of the moral life.

- St. Theophan the Recluse

St. Theophan the Recluse was one of the many
saints who lived in nineteenth-century Russia, during a
time of revival and fervor in Orthodox spirituality. St.
Theophan was both a scholar and a spiritual guide.
Much of the important literature we have in
translation, including *The Philokalia* and *Unseen Warfare*,
is the result of St. Theophan's translations.

Born in on January 10, 1815, he was given the name George Vasilievich Govorov. His parents were devout Christians. In fact, his father was a priest who was known for his piety. While George was young, it became apparent that he had a brilliant mind. Not only did he study religion but science and philosophy as well.

In 1841, at the age of 26, George attended Kiev Theological Academy, where he became a Master of Theology. After graduating, St. Theophan took monastic vows and was ordained into the priesthood. For a brief period, he was a professor at the seminary of Olonetz. Later he taught at the Academy of St. Petersburg.

In 1847 St. Theophan travelled to the Near East, visiting Syria, Egypt, Mount Athos, and Sinai. While travelling the saint discovered many valuable spiritual writings that were forgotten and left to decay in old monastery libraries. After finding these treasures, he began learning the languages of the manuscripts. He studied French, Hebrew, and Arabic, so that he might profit from their teachings. For seven years he journeyed the area and spent considerable time in Jerusalem. During his trip he learned Greek and immersed himself in the writings of the Fathers. When he returned he became rector of St. Petersburg Academy. In 1859, he became Bishop of Tambov; four years later he was appointed Bishop of Vladimir.

After seven years as bishop, he resigned and retired to the monastery of Vysha. In 1872 he withdrew to his cell, desiring to lead a life of solitude and prayer. During this time St. Theophan did much writing. Not only did he write several books, but he also corresponded with many people, receiving twenty to forty letters every day and answering each one. Further, as stated previously, he translated *The Philokalia* from church Slavonic into Russian, adding certain texts from the Syrian fathers. He also adapted and changed a Western work known today as *Unseen Warfare.*

After more than two decades of seclusion, St. Theophan died in his cell in 1894, at the age of 79. He was canonized in 1988, as part of the celebrations for the millennium of the Russian Orthodox Church. He left behind a body of work that includes teachings, correspondence, and translations that continue to instruct and encourage people today,

St. Theophan the Recluse is mostly known for his teachings on prayer. For him, prayer is not an activity for the morning and the evening. Prayer is a way of being. It is meant to be a constant state of existence. According to the Apostle Paul, "Pray without ceasing" (I Thes. 5:17). In the same way, St. Theophan believes that Christians should be in a constant state of communion. Our daily prayers are only a part of this way of living. He writes, "The final goal of man is communion with God." In fact, we were created for this reason. "God created man for a blessed existence—expressly to be lived in Him, and through living communion with him. For this reason, He breathed into man's nostrils the breath of life, that is, his spirit."

In *The Art of Prayer*, St. Theophan describes three states of communion. The first is simply the thought or intention. "Communion begins from the moment when hope of it is stimulated, and it shows itself on man's side in a yearning and aspiration towards God." Second, through the sacraments of baptism and confession, "the Lord enters into man by His grace, vividly establishes communion with him, and gives him a taste of all the sweetness of the Divine, as abundantly and intensely as those who have achieved perfection experience it." According to St. Theophan, God will then conceal this manifestation of communion, renewing it now and then, but usually as "merely a reflection" of the original.

Yet it is the third state that is the goal of the Christian life. At this third level, "the Lord perceptibly reveals His abode in a man's spirit, which then becomes a temple filled by the Three Persons of the Godhead." This state is not one that will be revealed only at the end of our labors; it is for the present and for each day of our lives. He states that "it must be our constant and unceasing state. When we have communion with God, and do not feel Him within us, we must recognize that we have turned away from our aim and from the way chosen for us." In other words, if we no longer sense the presence of God—His peace and joy—then our priorities are out of order.

Where does communion with God begin? St. Theophan writes, "A mystical communion with our Lord Jesus Christ is granted to believers in the holy sacrament of baptism." Being baptized is no guarantee, however, that we will be in communion with God. "All of us who have been baptized and chrismated, have received the gift of the Holy Spirit. He is in all of us, but He is not active in all of us."

We can even go through the rituals of prayer and the Divine Liturgy and still not be in communion with Him. St. Theophan states that

> cold obedience to the rules of the Church, legalistic action based on calculated reason, even punctuality, sobriety and honest behavior, are not in themselves absolute evidence that our life has a truly Christian quality.... All of these things are good, but as long as they are not informed by the spirit of life in Christ Jesus,

they have no value in the eyes of God. Then these acts are like lifeless idols. Good clocks run correctly, but who says they have life in them?

Thus, while baptism, chrismation, and all Christian works are essential to the spiritual life, they do not assure true communion with God.

How then do we attain such communion? The saint teaches us that we must first desire it. By desiring communion with God, we open ourselves to the possibility of receiving this spiritual gift. The key is not only to desire communion but to have a zeal for it. He writes, "Thus when we zealously desire constant communion with Him, God will bestow His grace upon us to help us attain our goal."

St. Theophan's third level of communion is not reached—or maintained—without a battle. As mentioned earlier, when our priorities get out of line and we do not place God first in our lives, then the communion is broken and we no longer sense His presence. He writes, "If we permit ourselves to stop short at specific aims an infinite inconstancy will come into our lives. Our lives should possess the one tone imparted by unity of aim, so that our entire life becomes a single sacrifice to God."

Close to the modern era, St. Theophan was aware of the internal as well as external distractions that take our attention away from our goal:

> On the thinking side you find confusion, distraction and wandering thoughts: on the desiring side instability, disorder and capricious desires. Our actions reflect this state. How much time we waste in idleness and empty activities! We roam hither and thither without knowing why. We do things again and again, without being able to give a sensible account of them. We take up one enterprise after another, and all that comes of it is fuss and bustle.

St. Theophan gives a good description of the modern life. We go places and do activities—many times in the name of the Lord—while forgetting the "one thing needful" (Luke 10:42).

What then is the solution? St. Theophan believes that we should do everything for the glory of God. When we have the attitude that each activity we do is one that should be done for God's glory, then we baptize our everyday existence with a sense of the sacred. If we are to be in constant communion with God, then we must approach our daily lives in no other way.

What St. Theophan saw in his own time, and is much truer today, is that we segment our lives so that our aim is pointed in too many directions. According to this saint, our one goal is communion with God. If we have several competing goals, it is no wonder that we feel divided and experience little or no communion. He writes,

> To do everything to the glory of God seems too strict for some people. They assume that in the affairs of the world one can have aims outside of God, if not actually excluding Him. Typically they say that, "We need to turn our souls to Him more often...." [T]his is simply laziness, which makes them reluctant to make real efforts to rise to God!... Lazy faces never shine with the light of Christ.

He later adds, "People say that other aims are permissible, so long as they do not exclude God, as if we were doing Him a favor by our acts. In fact, to say that all that is necessary is to dedicate a certain number of acts to Him is to imply that God is not truly concerned in the morality of life."

We see therefore that St. Theophan stresses that we must not divide our actions, some being for the kingdom, some being for our boss, and some being for our family. We must approach our everyday lives with the attitude that everything done this day will be done for God's glory. By doing so, we cultivate in our hearts an awareness of His presence throughout the day, and we become one step closer to attaining constant communion with God.

Part of the spiritual battle consists in guarding our hearts. We cannot have inner communion with God while at the same time harboring evil in our hearts. Thus we must keep watch, making sure that impurities do not enter our hearts. He explains, "Every influence that enters the should from outside is worked out by its thinking and acting functions, then settles in the heart. Whatever the soul manifests in the outside world first passes through the heart." In short, all evil actions begin in the heart. The goal is to keep our hearts from being contaminated by the world, thus keeping a holy temple in which our Lord may dwell.

St. Theophan teaches us to keep our thought on what is pure. He instructs that

> the thinking function seldom behaves as it should. It gives way to absent-mindedness, while the active part of us turns away from its proper direction in life and is seduced by changeable desire—desires aroused by alien passions, rather than soundly based on natural needs. This is why the heart finds no peace…. The dominant factor is that the heart is tyrannized by passions. If there were no passions we would still have to face things like dislike, but they would never torment the heart as the passions do.

In other words, when our heart is darkened by lust, envy, anger, and hatred, we have no peace. Inner turmoil breaks our communion with God. Elsewhere, he writes, "Against the inner sanctuary, where consciousness and freedom dwell, the enemy directs flaming arrows, attacking through the passions, and using our body and soul as places of ambush. But as long as freedom and consciousness remain unimpaired, firmly on the side of good, victory is ours."

St. Theophan warns us that the struggle is difficult. Some will be victorious; some will allow themselves to be defeated. "Anyone who enters the path of pleasing God with the help of grace, anyone who begins to strive towards God on the preordained path of Christ's law, risks being deflected at the crossroads." Yet he assures us that if we persevere we will have victory over our passions.

> After great and persistent effort, Christian principles will eventually emerge victorious and rule unopposed. They will enter every corner of human nature, dislodging every demand and inclination that opposes them. This makes it pure and dispassionate and worthy of the bliss of the pure in heart—so that they may see God in themselves by purest communion with Him.

We must therefore prepare our hearts, so that we can experience constant communion with Him.

Guarding the heart allows us to block evil thoughts before they take root. Moreover, it allows us to purify our hearts so communion may begin. St.

Theophan teaches that the Christian life consists of three stages: 1) turning to God; 2) purification or self-control; and 3) sanctification. The guarding of the heart falls under the second stage. It is the third stage that we experience constant communion with God, "the final goal of our labors and ascetic practices."

Through the development of our prayer life, the saint teaches that constant communion can be achieved. As stated previously, the communion that St. Theophan describes is different but not separate from our own prayer rule. For him, prayer is at the center of the Christian life:

> Where does life in God appear in all its fullness, power, and beauty? It appears at the highest levels of prayer, so great is the power of prayer and so high is its meaning…. He who knows how to pray is already saved. The field in which communion with God is formed and takes place is inner, spiritual prayer. The person praying is then at home in God—and as a result is very ready for God to make His home in him.

The importance of prayer in St. Theophan's writing cannot be ignored. One cannot have communion with God without developing a life of prayer.

In the book *The Path to Prayer*, St. Theophan gives us three types of prayer, in ascending order: spoken, mental, and unceasing prayer. Spoken prayer is simply our own personal rule of prayer: morning and evening prayers. He also includes in this category the prayers said in the Church. St. Theophan teaches us to focus on what we are doing, which is speaking to our Creator and Savior. We must listen therefore to the words we are saying. "If you say your prayers as you should, then you will inevitably awaken in yourself a rising up of the heart toward God—and this is the way to enter into the spirit of prayer."

This saint teaches us to use the prayer books of the Church as a guide. In them we learn from the masters: St. Macarius of Egypt, St. John Chrysostom, St. Basil the Great and others as well. St. Theophan instructs us that these prayers are God-inspired and their words are powerful. "By the law of reciprocal action, those who enter energetically and attentively into these prayers will taste the power of the original prayer to the extent that their spirit comes close to the spirit it contains."

In perfecting our spoken prayers, he gives us three suggestions. First, we must prepare ourselves for prayer. He writes,

> So, morning or evening, immediately before you begin to repeat your prayers, stand awhile, sit for a while, or walk a little and try to steady your mind and turn it away from all worldly activities and objects. After this, think who He is to whom you turn in prayer, then recollect who you are; who it is who is about to start this invocation to Him in prayer. Do this in such a way as to awaken in your heart a feeling of humility and reverent awe that you are standing in the presence of God.

This type of contemplation prior to prayer helps us to concentrate more fully on what we are saying. Moreover, it enables us to focus on the nature of our relationship with God.

Second, we must pay close attention to our spoken words. "Simply enter into every word and then bring the meaning down into your heart. That is, understand what you say, and then experience what you have understood." By proper attention, our prayer becomes more fruitful and effective. St. Theophan also instructs us on what to do when we lose concentration: "When our mind does in fact wander during prayer, recall it—and do so over and over again. Whenever you have said a prayer while your mind was wandering—and so have said it without feeling or comprehension—never forget to recite again all that you said in this way." By taking his advice, we are sure to make our prayers more effective (and perhaps a little longer).

His final rule for spoken prayer is that we not return to our usual activities immediately following our prayer. Instead, we should take a moment to contemplate what we have just experienced. "Stand for a while and consider what it is to which all this commits you. Try to hold in your heart what has been given to you to feel during prayer." He adds, "Nobody who has fulfilled his rule of prayer with care will immediately want to return to his ordinary interests."

In other words, for those of us in today's world, we should refrain from saying our prayers and then, say, turning on the television.

He warns us not to get bored with saying the same prayers. "Every repetition...will leave a mark of prayer on the soul. Uninterrupted practice in the order described will make it take root in your soul, and patience in this practice will establish a prayerful spirit."

Having learned and experienced spoken prayer—preparing ourselves, concentrating on the words, and contemplating their meaning for our lives—St. Theophan teaches that we are ready for mental prayer, the second of the three stages. At this stage we "attempt to bring something of our own to Him, so to speak; to raise ourselves toward Him; to open ourselves to Him; to confess to Him the contents and needs of our souls." Mental prayer proceeds therefore from spoken prayer. "Just in the same way that water pours of its own accord from an overfull vessel, so prayer to God begins to spring spontaneously from a heart which is filled with holy feelings that have been produced by the habit of regular vocal prayer."

It is possible, St. Theophan warns, to use a prayer book for years and never attain mental prayer. The reason is that

> the only time they make an effort to raise their hearts to God is while they are actually carrying out their rule of prayer…only in the morning, for example. They think that then their relationship is complete, their duty fulfilled. After this they spend their whole day in other activities, without ever turning to God. Then, when evening comes, they decide that it is time to turn back to the business of prayer.

Thus, when we remember God only during specific times of the day, we fail to achieve mental prayer, a deeper, purer communion with God.

The problem with such an approach is that the day's events become all-important to us and replace any thoughts of God. "So it happens that even if the Lord does give them a good disposition in the morning, it will be smothered under the fuss created by numerous activities of the day." Living this way causes the soul to harden, so that it has no desire to pray in the evening. Of such people, he writes, "They have lost control of themselves, and are unable to soften their souls even to a small degree, so that prayer does not come easily, nor ripen easily." How often have we experienced peaceful morning prayers, only to have the serenity dissipate upon entering morning rush hour traffic? After working all day, we enter back into the commute home and find ourselves spiritually spent by the evening.

To remedy this problem, "one must act in such a way that the soul does not turn to God only when…standing in prayer, but should do so as far as possible throughout the day. It should be an unceasing offering of oneself throughout the day." He suggests that we say short but frequent prayers during the day. For example, before beginning a task, one might say, "O Lord, bless us!" At its completion, we can say, "Glory be to Thee, O Lord." Of course, the best prayer to offer is the Jesus prayer ("Lord Jesus, Son of God, have mercy on me, a sinner") or variations of this prayer ("Lord have mercy"). This prayer also helps fight temptations that come to us throughout the day.

We must "attribute to Him our every activity, large or small." St. Theophan reminds us:

> If we give ourselves the task of fulfilling the apostolic command to do everything to the glory of God (I Cor. 10:31)—even eating and drinking—then we will inevitably remember God in whatever we do…and this not simply, but with circumspection, taking care that we do not act wrongly and do not trespass against God in any deed.

By turning to God with a short prayer, before and after each task, we keep Him at the front of our minds, allowing us to grow closer to the final stage—constant communion with God.

Meditation is another task that falls under the mental stage of prayer: "Meditation is another reverent reflection on godly attributes and action, and on what our glimpses of them demand of us." He suggests that we reflect on God's goodness, wisdom, justice, mercy, as well as the Holy Scriptures, the sacraments and the Kingdom of Heaven.

St. Theophan believes that the morning is the best time for meditation, after finishing morning prayers. At this time, "the soul is not yet burdened by a multitude of impressions and cares." He instructs us to sit after our morning prayers and reflect on one of the attributes of God. "Think about it so that it gives rise to similar attitudes in your own soul."

Thus, according to St. Theophan, to achieve the mental stage of prayer, three practices are helpful, if not necessary. First, we call out to God throughout the day, with brief appeals. Second, we must turn every action to the glory of God. Third, we should set aside a time to meditate on God and His attributes, preferably following our morning prayers.

These first two stage of prayer—spoken and mental—lead us to the third and final stage: constant communion with God (also referred to as unceasing prayer). The saint writes that this third stage "is genuine prayer for which the first two are merely preparations." It this type of prayer that "should abide in us as an uninterrupted state of the spirit, just as breathing and the beating of the heart are uninterrupted action of the body.

It is interesting to note that St. Theophan gives no step-by-step instructions as he did for the first two stages. For the most part, he reiterates the three steps of mental prayer but emphasizes the need to intensify them. For him, unceasing prayer is accomplished by turning constantly to God, so that He is not forgotten or lost in the hectic rush of our lives. He instructs us that once this stage is reached, it is "accompanied by inner warmth, and then by burning of the spirit." He writes:

> These three: reflection on God, doing everything to the glory of God, and frequent appeals to God, are the most effective tools for prayer of both mind and heart. Each moves the soul towards God. The labor this involves can be compared to climbing a mountain. The higher up the mountain one is, the lighter and easier does one breathe. It is the same here: the more one accustoms oneself to these exercises, the higher he will raise his soul; the higher the

soul rises, the more freely prayer will act within it.

We can see that mental prayer evolves into constant communion with God. At first, the inner warmth and burning spirit can be sensed briefly. With work and perseverance, these periods are extended, extended until it is a way of being.

Yet who can reach this final stage? According to St. Theophan, unceasing prayer can be achieved by all. He writes,

> Everyone sometimes feels a warmth and ardor during prayer. It happens when the soul becomes detached from everything, enters into itself, and so prays to God with real warmth. It is actually in this occasional inspired descent of the Spirit upon prayer that the landmark of prayer may be reached so that it becomes a constant condition.

Many Christians experience the "inner warmth" and "burning of the spirit" from time to time in their prayer lives. It is when this experience becomes a constant state that we know we are in constant communion with God and have achieved prayer without ceasing.

Thus, for St. Theophan the Recluse, communion with God is the goal of the Christian life. We attain communion through grace and our own work. Communion with God begins with our desire and yearning for God. Then, through baptism and chrismation, our awareness of God is deepened. These two stages are preludes to the state of constant communion with God, which is marked by "inner warmth" and a "burning of the spirit."

Communion can be deepened and furthered by the three types of prayer. The first type is spoken, as when saying the written prayers of the Church. This stage progresses to the second type, which is mental prayer. Here one continues with the spoken prayers but also calls out to God throughout the day. Another aspect of mental prayer is the meditation on the divine attributes. Then when we intensify all the above, we begin achieving unceasing prayer, that is a constant communion with God.

St. Theophan's teaching on this subject is charismatic in nature. He places much emphasis on the "feeling" we get when in communion with God. His instructions, however, are firmly rooted in the Eastern Christian tradition. His advice is directed to clergy, monastics, and laity alike. He managed to give practical instructions for achieving mystical states, not an easy task. Thus his gifts included not only the ability to reach exalted states of prayer, but also to instruct others on how they too may deepen their prayer lives.

Pray for us, St. Theophan, that, through our efforts and God's grace, we may achieve constant communion with God in this life.

Bibliography

Amis, Robin (editor and commentator). *The Heart of Salvation: The Life and Teachings of Saint Theophan the Recluse*. Translated by Ester Williams. Newbury, MA: Praxis Institute Press, 1992.

Chariton, Igumen (compiler). *The Art of Prayer: An Orthodox Anthology*. Translated by E. Kadloubovsky and E.M. Palmer. London: Faber and Faber, 1966.

Theophan the Recluse. *The Path of Prayer: Four Sermons on Prayer*. Translated by Ester Williams. Edited and compiled by Robin Amis. Newbury, MA: Praxis Institute Press, 1991.

Flames of Wisdom

IV

St. John of Kronstadt

On Prayer

People mostly pray as if there
were no God with them, or as if
He did not heed their prayers.
Let us ascribe to the Lord at
least the same amount of
attention that good parents
show to the requests of their
children, at least that provident
and attentive love which good
parents have for their children.

- St. John of Kronstadt

St. John of Kronstadt is one of the more
contemporary saints. He lived in northern Russia at the
end of the nineteenth and early twentieth-century. Like
our modern age, his time was an era of depravity,

doubt, and unbelief. The waves of Western atheism and agnosticism had begun to crash upon the shores of Russia. Social injustice was common. The rich became richer; the poor became poorer. Corruption and unbelief were seeping into the Church. In short, St. John faced many of the same dilemmas we face today.

In 1829, Ivan Ilyich Sergiev was born in the village of Suro in the Russian district of Pinega and was the son of a village subdeacon. Ordained parish priest of Kronstadt in 1855, where he would remain until his death in 1908, Father John became famous throughout Russia for his gifts of healing and pastoral care. Not only was he a great spiritual leader; he was a social reformer as well.

In 1851, Ivan Sergiev entered the St. Petersburg Theological Academy. At first the young man considered becoming a monk and going as a missionary to eastern Siberia. Instead he decided that his own people needed instruction and guidance, so he accepted an appointment at St. Andrew's Cathedral of Kronstadt where he served for the fifty-three years of his ministry.

He also married Elisaveta Konstantinovna, the daughter of the retired protopriest of the Kronstadt parish. (It should be noted that their marriage was never consummated. It was St. John's conviction that he should remain in a state of virginity. After some persuasion she agreed.)

Kronstadt was a rough town, filled with banished beggars and criminals. Stealing and begging were common in the streets of Kronstadt. But the saint was undaunted by these threats. He wandered through the streets, looking for people to help and encourage. Much to his wife's chagrin, he often gave away his pay before he was able to bring it home. Sometimes he would give away the shoes on his feet.

He rose early each morning to pray. Then he would go to the Cathedral, where he celebrated daily the Divine Liturgy. After the service he would make twelve to fifteen sick calls. People came from all over Russia to have him hear their confessions and pray for them.

St. John was greatly concerned about the poor of Kronstadt. At first he gave food and money to all who asked, but soon he saw that this practice was not only useless but harmful as well. In 1882, he founded the House of Industry, which was comprised of money. Through donations and grants, the House of Industry also provided free dinner and medical grants.

What is perhaps most amazing about St. John's activities is that they did not diminish his prayer life. In fact, one could say that prayer was his life and that his life was a prayer. Few saints, either modern or ancient, have blended the contemplative and the active life so well. Moreover, the distinction between active and contemplative blur in the life of St. John. His prayer life led to action and his actions led to more prayer.

In 1906, St. John's health began to decline. In 1908 he became seriously ill, though he continued to celebrate his daily Liturgy until December 10th of that year. He communicated daily until he fell into a coma the following week. On December 20th he received Communion for the last time. He died that morning.

St. John never wrote a systematic theology. His vast writings were all made as entries in his diary, which included his thoughts, prayers, and praises. The diary was later published as *My Life in Christ*. These writings give us both the struggles and victories of a godly man who managed to balance an active life with a contemplative one of prayer. As a priest (some called him the "pastor of all Russia"), he was concerned with his flock and with the many poor people who lived around him. He rose early for prayer and to administer the sacraments and could still be seen late into the night, visiting the sick and the despondent. His life was busy and hectic, but he baptized his activities in a strong life of prayer. His life is an example to all laity and priests who lead active and, at times, chaotic lives. And although he never systematized his writings, one theme runs like an undercurrent beneath the surface: the effectiveness of "correct" prayer.

First, St. John stresses the need for true faith when asking God for anything. He emphasizes the need to allow our words to sink into our hearts. St. John warns us that "if during prayer we pronounce the words disregarding their power, without feeling in our heart their truth, we shall not derive any benefit from the prayer, because true, faithful prayer must be in spirit and in truth." He also writes, "But for those who have not attained the capabilities of praying sincerely it is necessary to pray slowly, waiting for a corresponding echo in the heart to each word of the prayer. And this is not always soon given to men unaccustomed to prayerful contemplation." If we only relate to God with our lips, we are attempting to draw near to God with our flesh and not with our heart. Thus the emphasis is twofold: by praying slowly, concentrating on each word, our faith rises and, at the same time, we avoid the sin of hypocrisy.

Not only should we focus on our words in prayer, we should remember the One we are addressing. This may seem obvious; yet often our prayers are spoken haphazardly, without considering that we are speaking to our Lord, the Creator of the universe. St. John writes,

How small in proportion are all the other gifts which we ask of Him in prayer, and how easy it is for Him to give them to us at the first word of true faith, if they are really necessary for us! Therefore, it is perfectly unpardonable in us if we still doubt that we shall obtain what we ask of God in prayer. The Lord said plainly, "Ask and it shall be given you."

In Bishop Alexander's biography of St. John, he quotes him concerning this same theme:

Remember that whilst you pray God expects from you a positive answer to His question: "Do you believe I can fulfill your prayer?" You must be able to answer from the bottom of your heart: "Yes! I believe, oh God," and then you will be answered according to your faith. Remember that not one word is lost during prayer if you speak from your heart.

Thus, we must pray slowly, making sure our hearts are in accord with what we are saying; while, at the same time, we must believe—truly believe, by concentrating and not by flippantly entering into the light of His presence—and know God is able and is willing to give us all good things.

Second, St. John emphasizes the need for humility for effective prayer. His idea of humility does not include the unnecessary berating of ourselves before God; quite the contrary, he sees humility as stemming from a correct perspective of Creator and creation: from the Creator flows good things and to want more than what is given is sinful and indicative of an improper understanding of our relationship to God.

St. John warns against our desiring "lofty states of prayer," urging the reader to remember that such states come from God as He sees fit and that many such experiences happen in the lives of godly people who, through prayer and asceticism, have entered into a closer union with God. Bishop Alexander summarizes St. John's teaching on this subject: "we must not immediately aim to achieve lofty and unusual states of mind and think that, when praying in such a way, we are doing something special, peculiar only to the elect." Although "lofty" states of prayer may occur through asceticism and the purifying of passions, the believer must remember that such experiences still come ultimately from God. Losing this perspective opens the door to pride and self-righteousness.

We must also remember that "sweetness of prayer" is a gift from God, a gift after which we must not seek. Bishop Alexander explains: "According to the Fathers of the Church, sweetness of prayer is not to be achieved by man, it is God's gift, and during prayer we must not seek after it, but must only endeavor to eliminate everything that prevents us from being with God." The inexperienced Christian seeking after spiritual "experiences" can open up himself to an array of "sensations," which may be from a spirit, but not necessarily the Spirit of God. [1]

Like most Orthodox teachers he encourages the use of the Jesus Prayer as a way of acquiring humility, allowing us to pray simply and remain theologically correct. Once again, St. John emphasizes the need to pray the Jesus Prayer slowly and carefully. By practicing this simple prayer ("Lord Jesus Christ, Son of God, have mercy on me a sinner"), we are also given the strength to fight temptation.

In keeping with Orthodox tradition, St. John of Kronstadt reminds us that prayer is not to be understood as an individual act, apart from our union with other believers. In other words, our prayers should not consist of requests solely for ourselves, but also for those around us, especially for "those who belong to the family of believers"(Gal. 6:10).

Praying for others has a two-fold result: first and most obvious, our prayers are answered, benefiting and aiding those for whom we pray; the second outcome is an increasing love for both God and neighbor, the two being contingent upon one another. Bishop Alexander quotes St. John's teaching on this subject:

> Pray not only for yourself, but for all the faithful, for the whole body of the Church without separating yourself from other believers; pray in a state of union with them as a member of Christ's Church. . .. Prayer for others is beneficial for the one who prays: it purifies the heart, strengthens faith

and hope in God, and stimulates love
for God and neighbor.

In short, prayer benefits both the one who prays and the one for whom the believer is praying.

Once again, St. John urges us to pray sincerely and with conviction. He writes,

> Pray for the forgiveness of the sins of others as you pray for the forgiveness of your own; pray for the salvation of others as you pray for your own, and you will receive from God a wealth of spiritual gifts, the gifts of the Holy Spirit, Who loves a soul which is concerned with the salvation of others.

Thus the two-fold result of prayer is reiterated.

While praying for others in our personal prayers is of great importance, St. John, along with other Orthodox teachers, sees private prayers as preparatory to communal prayer, that is, prayers during the Divine Services. St. John writes, "Prayers at home are an introduction, a preparation for prayers in Church. Thus he who is not accustomed to pray at home can seldom pray diligently in Church. Experience bears witness to this: anyone can observe it for himself." Therefore, we may view our personal prayers as the fuel that feeds the fire of the liturgical prayers of the Church.

It should be clear by now the great importance St. John of Kronstadt placed on prayer. His life was permeated with the sweet fragrance that comes from a life of prayer and purity. Prayer, according to St. John, must be done each morning, each evening, and before any undertaking.

Concerning morning prayers, he writes, "In order to spend the day in a holy, peaceful and sinless way there is only one means: a sincere, ardent prayer in the morning on awakening. This prayer will introduce Christ with the Father and the Holy Spirit, into the heart and will give the soul strength and power to fight against sin." Knowing how hectic mornings can be, he empathizes with us but remains adamant: "Are you hurrying to work? Get up earlier, pray diligently and you will acquire tranquility, energy and success in work, for the whole day."

He also encourages us to pray each evening, regardless whether or not we are tired. He writes,

> When you pray at night do not forget to tell the Holy Spirit, with all sincerity and contrition, about all the sins which you have committed during the day....If you allow yourself to pray with diligence, you will not fall asleep before you have wept over your sins. Believe that, if for the sake of bodily rest, you pray hurriedly, you will lose the tranquility of both body and soul.

While it is important to pray morning and evenings, St. John had the wisdom to know that rigidity will do more harm than good: "Enforced prayer produces only hypocrisy, makes man listless even in the fulfillment of his duties, a slave to ritual, leading to Pharisaism and an insincere offering to God of an established rule."

He also realized that, whether through sickness or grief, often it is difficult to pray. With compassion and wisdom, he writes,

> When ill or suffering pain, or when overcome by grief, man, in the beginning, cannot have burning faith

or love for God, because during illness or sorrow the heart is aching, and faith and love require a healthy, calm heart: therefore we must not be too sorry if during illness or grief we are not able to pray and to love God as we should. There is a time for everything. Even for prayer, it is sometimes the wrong time.

Obviously, St. John saw this period as a temporary state; but, nevertheless, his counsel echoes with wisdom, compassion, and a realistic knowledge of our human weaknesses. It should be noted, too, that his biographer tells us that St. John was much easier and sympathetic toward his flock than he was toward himself.

Hence, to lead an effective Christian life, we should pray mornings to prepare us for the day, and evenings so that we might confess our sins, preparing our bodies and souls for sleep. During the day, as stated previously, the Jesus Prayer is an excellent way to keep Christ in the front of our minds and to receive divine assistance. St. John writes, "It is indispensable for every Christian to acquire the habit of turning quickly to God in prayer about everything." Before undertaking any work, we should pray to God: "Jesus, help me! Jesus, enlighten me! Thus your heart will be supported and warmed by lively faith and hope in Christ."

St. John's teachings on prayer are vast, as are his other spiritual counsels. Yet certain themes recur: pray with sincere faith and humility, uttering our words carefully and thoughtfully; pray for others as well as ourselves; by doing so we acquire greater love for God and our neighbor while at the same time benefiting the recipient of our supplications; and finally, pray mornings, evenings, and prior to any undertaking, using the Jesus Prayer throughout the day. We must remember that while stressing the importance of prayers, St. John knew the dangers of a rigid plan for prayer; he also knew that at certain times in our lives, praying might be difficult, if not impossible. During periods of grief or sickness we must not feel guilty or ashamed, but remember that "there is a time for everything." We can offer to God our sufferings and deprivations as a prayer to Him.

St. John of Kronstadt was certainly a saint for the modern age. His teachings provide answers to our troubled, complex post-Christian world. As stated earlier, he never wrote a systematic theology; his writings were not solely for the learned, but for every person attempting to lead a life of faith in a world of unbelief. Although he was well-educated, his wisdom was of an existential nature, the type not learned from books. By reading his words we can draw on his wisdom to lead a Christian life in a non-Christian world.

St. John, pray that we too may learn to pray in this age of doubt and unbelief.

Notes

1. St. Seraphim Rose's book, *Orthodoxy and The Religion of the Future* (St. Herman of Alaska Brotherhood: Platina, CA, 1990) explores the possibility of spiritual deception for the believer who is seduced by the temptation for "lofty" experiences.

Bibliography

Alexander, Bishop (Semenoff-Tian-Chansky). *The Life of Father John of Kronstadt.* Crestwood, New York: St. Vladimir's Seminary Press, 1979.

Sergieff, John Iliytch (of Kronstadt). *My Life in Christ.* Translated by E. E. Goulaeff. Jordanville, NY: Holy Trinity Monastery (printshop of St. Job of Pochaev), 1984.

V

St. Isaac the Syrian
On Reading Scripture

Always consider yourself as needing instruction so that you may be found wise throughout your life.

- St. Isaac of Nineveh

Those who come from Protestant backgrounds often display a great zeal for the reading of Scripture. While Orthodox believers might be rightfully cautious about the individual interpretations to which such readings are so prone, one should not infer that the Orthodox faith downplays the importance of reading the Holy Scriptures. Perhaps no Orthodox saint better displays the zeal for Scriptures as does St. Isaac the Syrian.

Little is known of this saint's life, but his love for reading the Scriptures is an inspiration for all Orthodox believers. Consecrated Bishop of Nineveh (ca. 660-680), St. Isaac, after only five months, asked to withdraw so that he might live as a hermit in Bet Huzaje. Finally, he went to a monastery in Iran, where he studied Scripture so diligently that he became blind and had to dictate his writings, which may account for the difficulty of his style. Throughout his teachings, the importance of Scripture reading appears again and again.

According to St. Isaac the study of Scripture is important for several reasons. First, he warns that we should not approach Scripture with the intent of gaining intellectual knowledge:

> For education in your way of life, do
> not look at the sentences laid down
> for examination--as those who are

trained by teachers do--so that your soul is exalted by the importance of the considerations which are in them. Rather distinguish the meaning of the word in all the stories that you find in the Scriptures, that you may deepen your soul to dwell with the great insights which are in the statements of those who are illumined.

Thus St. Isaac encourages us not to seek knowledge that "puffs up" (I Cor. 8:1). Instead, we should approach Scripture in a more contemplative way: "Contemplation [theoria] is the perception of the divine mysteries hidden in the things which are spoken [in the Scriptures]."

St. Isaac teaches us how we should read these Sacred texts. First, we must approach the them with much reverence and prayer: "Do not approach the words of the mysteries contained in the divine Scriptures without prayer and beseeching God for help, but say: Lord, grant me to perceive the power in them! Reckon prayer to be the key to the true understanding of the divine Scriptures." Second, we must set aside a time of silence, so that our full concentration will be focused on what we are reading. He writes, "Let your reading be done in complete stillness, when you are freed from excessive care of the body and the tumult of affairs." Then our reading will give our souls "a delightful taste of sweet understandings, beyond the senses." We must find therefore a quiet time in our day to study the Bible. Beginning with prayer, we ask God for help in understanding His precepts and teachings. Then he aids our understanding as we meditate on the words, allowing them to sink into our soul, thus transforming and renewing our hearts and minds and leading us on the path to purity. Remember that prayer is the key to our understanding!

Each of us must find that special quiet time for our Bible reading and prayer. While morning and evening are preferred, St. Isaac teaches us that it is good to read the divine Scriptures just before going to sleep. He states,

> Let us then be diligent, my brethren,
> and long before we wish to go to sleep
> let us ponder upon the glorifications
> and our psalm-singing and our reading

from the holy Scriptures, keeping our soul from evil recollections and from every odious reflection and let us furnish our treasury with every sort of beautiful thing. Then sleep will overtake us while we are full of the recollection of God, and our soul will be aflame with ardent longing for the good things. . . because God's grace surrounds us in our sleep and pours forth upon us its gifts, though we slumber.

We see St. Isaac's two-fold purpose for reading the Scriptures just before we sleep: One, it keeps our minds from evil recollections, replacing them with thoughts of God and "every sort of beautiful thing." Second, reading before we sleep will cause our soul to long for the things of God; for though we sleep His grace will surround us.

According to St. Isaac, "The beginning of the way of life consists in applying the mind to the words of God." He also states, "In laying the foundation of virtue, the first of its peculiar elements is when we withdraw ourselves in flight from things toward the luminous word of the straight and holy paths, that word which was called an enlightener by the Psalmist inspired by the Holy Spirit."[1] Once again, St. Isaac encourages us to "withdraw ourselves in flight from things." This passage is similar to a previous one where he tells us to be "freed from excessive care" when studying the Scriptures. He emphasizes single-mindedness because of the importance he places on the reading of Scripture in the Christian life. He believes, along with the Psalmist, that the words of God are a lamp unto our feet (Ps. 119:105); therefore, we should approach the Scriptures as one willing to be taught, while, at the same time, making sure our understanding of what we read conforms to the teachings of the Church.

Another advantage of reading Scripture is that it banishes bad thoughts and habits. St. Isaac writes, "Nothing can so banish licentious habits from the soul and restrain memories which disturb and stir up troubling flames in the body as can avid devotion to the love of learning and searching investigation into the meanings of the passages of Scripture." He also states,

Burden the soul with the labor of reading the Scriptures which make known the narrow ways of ascetic life and of contemplation, as well as the stories of the saints; that you may exchange one habit for another even if in the beginning your soul does not feel pleasure because of the thick darkness and confusion of present memories. Then when you arise for prayer and for the office, instead of musing upon things of the world, ideas from Scripture will be imprinted in the mind. And with these, the memory of what it already has seen and heard will be effaced from it. In this way your mind will come to purity.

Not only are bad memories replaced but, by reading the Scriptures, we are led to the path of purity. This same idea is expressed elsewhere in St. Isaac's works:

If you desire chastity restrain the flow of base thoughts by occupying yourself with the study of the lections [of Scripture] and in continuous intercession before God. Then you will be armed within, against occasions [of sin] from nature. Otherwise you cannot discern purity within yourself.

Consequently, Christians will be purified, and they will see the purity within themselves. In other words, Scripture enables us to discern the purities and impurities of the heart. St. Isaac writes that without the constant reading of Scripture, "subtlety of thoughts is not learned."

But what is purity? According to St. Isaac, purity of mind is different from purity of the heart. He writes,

> The mind indeed with a little study of the Scriptures and a little labor in fasting and stillness forgets its former musing and is made pure, in that it becomes free from alien habits. It is also easily defiled. The heart, however, is purified with great sufferings and by being deprived of all mingling with the world, together with complete mortification in everything.

Yet St. Isaac warns that purity, from reading the Scriptures and from asceticism, whether of the mind or of the heart, does not come easily. He writes that "every purification which is achieved easily, quickly and with little labor is easily defiled. But the purity acquired with great troubles over a long period and by the highest part of the soul does not fear insignificant contacts with worldly things."

This advice is something to which we should hold on. In an age that emphasizes instant answers and quick service, we should understand that such modern day "virtues" do not pertain to the Christian life. Purity must be sought, but not expected too quickly. St. Isaac teaches us: "Everything which is readily found is also easily lost. Everything which is gained with labor is guarded with vigilance."

As St. Isaac has told us, the Scriptures play a fundamental role in the daily Christian life. They cannot be divorced, however, from the life of the Church and its members. Nor can spiritual knowledge be gained from the Scriptures alone. St. Isaac tells us, "Spiritual knowledge is a consequence of the practice of good works. Both are preceded by love and fear." The life of the Church encompasses all that brings us to purity and godliness: holy tradition (of which Scripture is a part), the Divine Liturgy, and of course the Holy Mysteries. Living in the fullness of the Church, persevering in the race and fighting the good fight, must include the Scriptures as well as all other aspects contained in the life of the Church.

St. Isaac never downplays the difficulty of the Christian life. It is a fight and a struggle. As Jesus told his disciples, "And from the days of John the Baptist until now the kingdom of heaven suffereth violence, and the violent take it by force" (Matt. 11:12). But while the Christian life may be difficult, St. Isaac offers encouragement by reminding us that God lives within us and He is not difficult to find:

> It is not necessary to roam heaven and earth after God or to send our mind to seek Him in different places. Purify your soul, O son of man, remove from yourself the thought of memories outside of nature; hang the veil of chastity and humility before your impulses. By means of these you will be able to find Him who is within you.

Since God lives within each baptized Christian, St. Isaac encourages us to do away with all that hinders our sight of Him. And, as we have seen, the Scriptures serve to purify and, in part, enable us to understand ourselves and the kingdom of God.

Accordingly, St. Isaac gives us clear reasons for reading the Scriptures. When they are understood in the context of the Church and not at the level of individual interpretation, the Scriptures purify and enlighten us. While the struggle for purity is difficult, St. Isaac has given us instruction on how to fulfill our goal. Above all, he encourages us to seek our Lord and to be single-minded: "Thirst for Jesus, that He may intoxicate you with His love. Close your eyes to the precious things of the world that you may deserve to have the peace of God reign in your heart."

Pray for us, St. Isaac, that our zeal for the reading of Scripture be increased and our understanding deepened.

Notes

1. Psalms 25:10 and 119:105

Bibliography

St. Isaac of Nieveh. *The Ascetical Homilies of St. Isaac the Syrian.* Brookline, MA: Holy Transfiguration Monastery, 1984.

St. Isaac of Nieveh. *On Ascetical Life.* Translated by Mary Hansbury. Crestwood, New York: St. Vladimir's Seminary Press, 1989.

VI

St. Dorotheos of Gaza
On Humility

Nothing is more powerful than humility.

- St. Dorotheos

Little is known about the life of St. Dorotheos of Gaza. Only by piecing together information from his many discourses have scholars been able to compose a picture of this saint's life. Even so, the picture is less than clear.

It is estimated that St. Dorotheos was born in the early sixth century, in Antioch. At that time Antioch was a diverse city. Much of the population embraced the Christian faith, while a good portion remained pagan. Within the city was also a strong

Jewish colony. We know from the words of St. John Chrysostom that, a century earlier, Antioch was a sensual, pleasure-loving city.

From various comments made in his discourses, we can assume that Dorotheos learned to read at a young age and was quite studious. It is thought that he attended a Christian school of rhetoric in Gaza and may have been a professor at one of the academies in Gaza. While it is unknown how much time was spent there, it must have been long enough to develop a reputation for himself, which would explain why his name is connected to that city. Regardless, judging from his wide range of references, from Aristotle to the Fathers, we can assume he was a well-educated man.

St. Dorotheos began his monastic life at Thawatha, two miles southwest of Gaza, where he eventually became a spiritual director and later was installed as the abbot of the community. At the time of St. Dorotheos's arrival, two well-known saints, Sts.

Barsanufius and John, lived as hermits at Thawatha. In fact, these men discipled him, mostly through letters of admonition.

We can also assume that St. Dorotheos was rather unhealthy, judging from some of his comments concerning his difficulty in maintaining the ascetic practices of the community. It is estimated that he died at a relatively young age, sometime around the year 560. To this day his remains have not been found.

Some scholars believe that he formed an independent community after the death of St. Barsanufius; others believe he remained at Thawatha, but moved from one area of the monastic complex to another, from the common life to a solitary one.[1] What is evident, however, is that St. Dorotheos was a man who lived and died quietly, always shadowed by the fame of Sts. Barsanufius and John. Thus what better saint to teach us the importance of humility.

For St. Dorotheos true humility is of supreme importance. It is the virtue that brings grace to the soul and causes our lives to bear much fruit. Not only does humility produce joy and peace in our lives; it also protects us from the passions. Humility is something rooted deep within our souls. True humility "is not humble in word or outward appearance but is deeply planted in the very heart."

But what is true humility? He first teaches us what it is not: "self-justification, this holding fast to our own will, this obstinacy in being our own guide. All this was the product of that hateful arrogance toward God." Then he goes on to describe humility: "Whereas the products of humility are self-accusation, distrust of our own sentiments, hatred of our own will. By these one is made worthy of being redeemed, of having his human nature restored to its proper state."

The saint teaches that two types of pride and two types of humility exist. He states, "The first kind of pride is when a man despises his brother, considers him worth little or nothing, while he puts a much greater value on himself. Such a man, unless he speedily repents and takes great care, will come in a short time to that second kind of pride by which he lifts himself up against God, and ascribes what he does right not to God, but to himself." Hence, if we see ourselves as superior to others, we are in danger of taking the next step, which is to see ourselves as independent from God. And, for St. Dorotheos, there is not a wide chasm between the two. The first proceeds naturally into the latter.

In much the same way, the saint teaches that there are two types of humility:

> The first kind of humility is to hold my brother to be wiser than myself, and in all things to rate him higher than myself, and simply...to put oneself below everyone. The second kind is to attribute to God all virtuous actions. This is the perfect humility of the saints. It is generated naturally in the soul by the performance of the commandments.

As we can see, the two types of humility are conversely related to his two types of pride. Moreover, he teaches us that obeying the commandments produces humility.

The importance of humility is central to St. Dorotheos' teachings. It is the prerequisite for bearing fruit in the Christian life. He states,

> There are certain kinds of trees which never bear fruit as long as their branches stay up straight, but if stones are hung on the branches to bend them down they begin to bear fruit. So it is with the soul. When it is humbled it begins to bear fruit, and the more fruit it bears the lowlier it becomes. So also the saints: the nearer they get to God, the more they see themselves as sinners.

In fact, he also says, "Any virtue existing without humility is no virtue at all."

By being humble, St. Dorotheos taught that we not only protect ourselves from the passions, but we also gain peace, a peace that passes all understanding (Phil. 4:7). This peace comes from our ability to combat the passions through our humility. He explains this connection in the following way:

> In point of fact there is nothing more powerful than lowliness. If a painful experience comes to a humble man, straightway he goes against himself, straightway he accuses himself as the one worthy of punishment, and he does not set about accusing anyone or putting the blame on anyone else. For the rest, he goes on his way untroubled, undepressed, in complete peace of mind, and as he has no cause to get angry or to anger anyone else. And so you see, the holy man quite rightly said, 'Before anything else we need humility.'

In other words, if we have true humility, we gain a certain peace of mind, because we are no longer concerned with defending ourselves or our actions, nor are we looking to blame or accuse someone else. The truly humble person accepts accusations with a quiet, unassuming response.

What St. Dorotheos is admonishing us to do is to live our daily lives with "lowliness of mind." He states, "Live through lowliness of mind instead of going to your death through pretentious pride." In his discourses we find two distinct ways in which this humility of the mind is manifested. The first way is our willingness to accept instruction; the second is our attitude toward our neighbor.

St. Dorotheos warns us that "we should not set ourselves up as guide posts, that we should not consider ourselves sagacious, that we should not believe we can direct ourselves. We need assistance, we need guidance in addition to God's grace." It takes humility to admit that we need help and guidance. It also means going against the American belief which places individualism on such a high pedestal. How many times have we heard, whether on talk shows or in our everyday conversations, remarks such as "It should be left up to the individual" or "Whatever is right for that person is what that person should do"? This attitude, so prevalent in our society, would be appalling to the saint. For him such statements are the epitome of pride.

The Christian who has true humility realizes that God uses others to help clarify His will for each person. St. Dorotheos wisely asks, "For how can we know the will of God or seek it completely if we believe only in ourselves and hold on to our own will?" When seeking God's will we must not only turn to the Scriptures and the writings of the Holy Fathers, but we must also ask the advice of those whose experiences in the faith have taught them so much. To lean on one's own understanding without seeking counsel is to fall into the devil's hands: "Such people the devil loves and he always rejoices over them, the ungoverned, those who are not subject to one who has power, under God, to help them and to give them a hand." In short, if in humility we ask for another's help, we allow ourselves to receive both the counsel and the encouragement needed to live the Christian life.

Second, our attitude toward our neighbor says much about our "lowliness of mind." As mentioned earlier, seeing ourselves as superior to others is the first type of pride. Anytime we judge our neighbor we place ourselves above that person. St. Dorotheos warns us: "Those who want to be saved scrutinize not the shortcomings of their neighbor but always their own and they set about eliminating them. Such was the man who saw his brother doing wrong and groaned, 'Woe is me; him today—me tomorrow'. " More importantly, we have no way of knowing the heart of the person. Perhaps we see someone sinning. He asks us, "And how do you know what tears he has shed about it before God? You may well know about the sin, but you do not know about the repentance." If we are truly humble, we will not judge our neighbor. We should be too aware of our own weaknesses and, not knowing the heart of our neighbor, choose instead to accuse only ourselves.

How can we attain this kind of humility? First, it is a gift from God, one for which we must pray, asking God to grant us the spirit of humility. Being the practical man that he was, St. Dorotheos offers some good advice on how we may gain this "lowliness of mind." By denying ourselves small pleasures, he teaches that we lose our sense of entitlement, the belief that we deserve a little extra: "For through certain small and worthless things our inordinate desires bind us again to the world without our realizing it. If, therefore, we desire to be set free and enjoy perfect freedom, let us learn to cut off our desires and so, with God's help, in a little while, we shall make progress and arrive at a state of tranquility."

By cutting off our desire for more, we train ourselves to be content with less. We live in a society where people clamor about their rights being violated, and others never feel they are getting their fair share. Truly humble people accept their lot and ask for no more. This does not mean that we should accept the social injustices and inequities that are inflicted on others; what it does mean, however, is that we must strive toward personal humility, which in turn would exalt others. While society will have always its victims, we, as Christians, should acquire an attitude that will be so "selfless" that we accept our own given circumstances while not being complacent about the deprivations of others.

What St. Dorotheos suggests is that we learn to deny ourselves the little pleasures in which we often indulge ourselves. When we learn to say no to another helping of dessert or to some item we may want to purchase, we begin training ourselves to become humble people. Allowing someone to go before us while in line at a store or restaurant instills in our hearts that others are more important or, at least, allows us to die to our desire to be first. St. Dorotheos teaches us: "A man denying himself in this way comes little by little to form a habit of it, so that from denying himself in little things, he begins to deny himself in great [things] without the least trouble." Accordingly, denying our own wants and desires is the beginning of the path to humility.

St. Dorotheos believed that humility is planted deep within the soul. Without it we would be unable to bear fruit or do any virtuous act. Humility brings us peace; for when we are humble we are not competing with others or worried and angered over what someone has said or done to us. He teaches that if we are truly humble, we will seek counsel from others and will refuse to judge our neighbor. And by renouncing our small desires, we will learn the way to humility. The saint gives us these words of encouragement: "we are not yet perfect, but at least we desire to be so, and this is the beginning of salvation."

Pray for us, St. Dorotheos, that we may attain humility in this life, that we may be perfected in the next.

Notes

1.   For a summary and a fuller explanation of the disagreement about whether St. Dorotheos founded a community or stayed at Thawatha, see the introduction by Eric P. Wheeler to *Dorotheos of Gaza: Discourses and Sayings* (60-67). Translated by Eric P. Wheeler. Kalamazoo, Michigan. Cisterican Publications, 1977.

Bibliography

Wheeler, Eric T., trans. *Dorotheos of Gaza: Discourses and Sayings.*Kalamazoo, Michigan: Cistercian Publications, 1977.

VII

St. John Climacus

On Controlling the Tongue

For the man who recognizes his sins has taken control of his tongue, while the chatterer has yet to discover himself as he should.

- St. John Climacus

Like many of the early saints, little is known of St. John Climacus, also known as St. John of the Ladder. He is widely known for his classic work, *The Ladder of Divine Ascent*. Much of what we do know comes from his own writing.

In Bishop Kallistos Ware's introduction to *The Ladder*, we find that John Climacus was probably born shortly before 579 and died around 649. He was sixteen years old when he came to the monastic community at Sinai. John was tonsured as a monk when he was nineteen or twenty.

At an early age he was recognized as a great spiritual guide. In fact, the stream of visitors he received caused many to criticize him, calling him a gossip and a "chatterbox." When hearing this John remained totally silent for one year, until his former critics urged him to speak once more.

Shortly after this incident, St. John lived forty years in solitude, at a place called Tholas. He was elected against his will as abbot of the great monastery of Mount Sinai. During this period of his life, he was asked by the superior of a monastery at Raithu to compose a book of instruction for the monks. The end result was *The Ladder of Divine Ascent*. Having completed this great work, he later resigned as abbot, longing for solitude again. He appointed his brother, George, as a replacement. John died shortly after leaving his position.

The importance of *The Ladder* cannot be overstated. While written especially for monastics, it is a book from which spiritual guidance can be attained by anyone desiring to grow in the Christian life. From an ascetic standpoint, the book is often severe. Yet it has earned a place in the history of monasticism that few other works have managed to do. Ware writes,

> With the exception of The Bible and the service books, there is no work in Eastern Christendom that has been studied, copied and translated more often than The Ladder of Divine Ascent by St. John Climacus. Every Lent in Orthodox monasteries it is appointed to be read aloud in church or in the refectory, so that some monks will have listened to it as much as fifty or sixty times in the course of their life.

Ware also notes that the work has been widely read by lay people in Greece, Bulgaria, Serbia, and Russia. He compares its popularity in the East to that of *The Imitation of Christ* in the West.

St. John's ladder consists of thirty steps, each one ascending to the next level of the spiritual life. Much of *The Ladder* is filled with picturesque images, clothed in a style that is at times abrupt as well as humorous. Of the thirty steps only three are directly related to the tongue. Slander, talkativeness, and falsehood are the three steps that deal directly with this subject. What he teaches us is as pertinent today as it was nearly fifteen hundred years ago.

According to the saint, the whole body needs to be in complete submission to God. For example, we must control our eyes from lust, the stomach from gluttony, and the ears from listening to gossip. In the same way, the tongue must be restrained. This view is corroborated by Scripture. St. James warns, "If any one considers himself religious and yet does not keep a tight rein on his tongue, he deceives himself and his religion is useless" (Jas. 1:26 NIV).

He teaches us that we must avoid the sin of talkativeness. Scripture teaches us, "When words are many, sin is not absent, but he who holds his tongue is wise" (Prov. 10:19 NIV). John tells us what is at the root of this sin. "Talkativeness results from a bad or relaxed life-style . . . or it comes from vain glory, a particular problem with ascetics; or it comes from gluttony, which is why many who keep a hard check on the stomach can more easily restrain the blathering tongue." It makes sense that if, through ascetic practices such as fasting, we learn to use self-control in one area, it should become less difficult for us to restrain other passions.

Expounding on vainglory as one of the roots of this sin, he writes, "Talkativeness is the throne of vainglory on which it loves to preen itself and show off." In a typical passage from The Ladder, he warns us where talkativeness leads: "Talkativeness is a sign of ignorance, a doorway to slander, a leader of jesting, a servant of lies, the ruin of compunction, a summoner of despondency, a messenger of sleep, a dissipation of recollection, the end of vigilance, the cooling of zeal, the darkening of prayer." In short, talkativeness endangers the soul.

It is not that we must take vows of silence or sit mute at all times. The saint teaches us that we must take control over what we say, thinking before speaking. This restraining of the tongue can only be accomplished by being sober-minded. Like many of the Fathers, John instructs us to remember our own mortality, our own death, as a way of conquering the sins of the tongue. We must remember the words of Christ: "I tell you, on the day of judgment men will render an account for every careless word they utter; for by your words you will be justified, and by your words you will be condemned" (Matt. 12:36-37). St. John writes, "The man who is seriously concerned about death reduces the amount of what he has to say, and the man who has received the gift of spiritual mourning runs from talkativeness as from a fire."

If talkativeness can endanger the soul, it follows that silence can offer healing and renewal. St. John writes,

> Intelligent silence is the mother of prayer, freedom from bondage, custodian of zeal, a guard on our thoughts, a watch on our enemies, a prison of mourning, a friend of tears, a sure recollection of death, a painter of judgment, . . . a companion of stillness, the opponent of dogmatism, a growth of knowledge, a hand to shape contemplation, hidden progress, the secret journey upward.

In other words, silence brings the converse of talkativeness. If talkativeness causes us to sin and draw away from God, then silence is the remedy that nurtures prayer and the sweet remembrance of the holy and divine.

Not only do we draw closer to God through silence; we also prevent ourselves from falling into sin. "The lover of silence draws close to God. He talks to him in secret and God enlightens him. Jesus, by His silence, shamed Pilate; and a man, by his stillness, conquers vainglory."

Therefore, when we are in the presence of others, we should not always think about what we should say next. Moreover, we must weigh our words, asking ourselves if what we want to say will benefit the listener. Are we wanting to speak in order to slander another, to make ourselves look better? Or are we wanting to say something that will show how intelligent or "spiritual" we are? We must consider our motives before we speak.

Another sin which is born of the tongue is slander. St. John defines slander as "the offspring of hatred, a subtle and yet crass disease, a leech in hiding and escaping notice, wasting and draining away the lifeblood of love. It puts on the appearance of love and is the ambassador of an unholy and unclean heart."

The reason this saint sees slander as subtle and as "hiding and escaping notice" is because often slander hides in a cloak of so-called virtue. How often have we repeated a story about someone under the guise of "concern" for another? If we have, St. John teaches us to reconsider.

> If, as you insist, you love that man, then do not be making a mockery of him, but pray for him in secret, for this is the kind of love that is acceptable to the Lord. And remember—now I say this as something to be pondered, and do not start passing judgment on the offender— Judas was one of the company of Christ's disciples and the robber was in the company of killers. Yet what a turnabout there was when the decisive moment arrived!

While we are repeating the sin to another, the person who committed the sin may be weeping before God.

Slander is closely related to judging, if not condemning others. St. John warns us: "To pass judgment on another is to usurp shamelessly a prerogative of God, and to condemn is to ruin one's soul." He also writes, "Do not make judgments, and you will travel no quicker road to the forgiveness of sins." Because we know not the hearts of others, he teaches us that judging others is incompatible to the Christian life of repentance. He writes,

> Fire and water do not mix; neither can you mix judgment of others with the desire to repent. If a man commits a sin before you at the very moment of his death, pass no judgment, because the judgment of God is hidden from men.

It has happened that men have sinned greatly in the open but have done greater deeds in secret, so that those who would disparage them have been fooled, with smoke instead of sunlight in their eyes

He further warns that "whatsoever sin of body or spirit that we ascribe to our neighbor we will surely fall into ourselves."

While we have a responsibility to correct a fallen member of the Church, we must do so only after praying and receiving guidance. Moreover, it must be done with the proper attitude. St. John relates to us his own experience: "I knew a man who sinned openly but repented in secret. I denounced him for being lecherous but he was chaste in the eyes of God, having propitiated Him by a genuine conversion." In other words, we are responsible for our brother and sister in Christ; yet if they sin we must approach them in love. We have no excuse when we go to another and describe the shameful deed, even when it is done in the name of "concern." We have no capacity for judging another's heart; nor do we have the responsibility to inform others of someone's sin. Once again, prayer for the fallen person is what is needed. Then, after prayer and guidance, we may approach the person with humility and attempt to guide the person back to the path of righteousness.

St. John Climacus advises those who struggle with the sin of slander to blame the demons responsible for another's sinful behavior. "If you want to overcome the spirit of slander, blame not the person who falls but the prompting demon." By blaming the "prompting demon" the sin is referred back to the one with whom sin originated.

Another way of overcoming the sin of slander is to look for the good in the one who committed the particular sin. He writes,

> A good grape picker chooses to eat ripe grapes and does not pluck what is unripe. A charitable and sensible mind takes careful note of the virtues it observes in another, while the fool goes looking for faults and defects. It is of such a one that it was said, "They have searched out iniquity and died in the search" (Ps. 63:7).

Thus we must look for the good in others and not find fault.

Not only must we refrain from slandering, but we must avoid listening to it also. Whether at work or in some other public place, we often listen to gossip and slander, not wanting to offend the speaker. John warns us that we must desist in this practice.

Do not allow human respect to get in your way when you hear someone slandering his neighbor. Instead, say to him: "Brother, stop it! I do worse things every day, so how can I criticize him?" You accomplish two things when you say this. You heal yourself and you heal your neighbor with one

135

bandage. Also, by doing so, we increase our humility by realizing our own sinfulness.

St. John Climacus gives us advice that transcends the many years that have passed since his words were first written. He instructs us, in accordance with Scripture, that the tongue, like all members of the body, must be tamed. His teachings encourage us to look for the hidden motive of what we are saying about another. Are we repeating gossip we have heard so that we may feel better about ourselves? Are we speaking out of our own pride, believing that no such sin could ever be committed by us?

He warns us that talkativeness often causes us to sin, while silence draws us closer to God. He also sees how easy it is to repeat slander under the guise of "concern." He tells us instead to look at our own faults and pray for those who sin. In this way we will not be guilty of judging others, a sin linked closely to slander.

Not only should we refrain from speaking badly about others; we must also refuse to listen to slander or accusations. St. John teaches us to spend more time looking for the good in others, ignoring the weaknesses and always remembering that we too are capable of the same sins.

By practicing the teaching of St. John Climacus, we will understand the importance and the difficulty of taming the tongue.

Pray for us, St. John Climacus, that we may take seriously the words we speak and, by God's grace, increase our mastery over the tongue.

Bibliography

Climacus, John. *The Ladder of Divine Ascent.*
    Translated by Colm Luibheid and Norman
    Russell. Introduction by Kallistos Ware.
    Ramsey, NJ: Paulist Press, 1982.

VIII

St. Tikhon of Zadonsk

On Struggling Against Sin

There is no victory more glorious than to
be victorious over one's self and sin.
There is no crown or triumph without
victory, and no victory without struggle
against enemies.

- St. Tikhon of Zadonsk

St. Tikhon of Zadonsk was born into extreme
poverty in 1724, in a Russian province of Novgorod.
His given name at birth was Timofey Sokolov. In fact,
he could not even attend school until age 15, when he
had earned the required money by digging vegetable
plots.

After his studies, young Timofey became a monk and it was then, in 1758, that he received the name Tikhon. In 1761, at the age of 38, he became bishop of Keksholm and Ladoga. All this time, however, his one desire was for a life of solitary asceticism. It did not help matters that the times were difficult: Western secularism was leaving its mark on the land; moreover, the diocese he oversaw was filled with high absenteeism, drunken priests, or those who had taken the position only as a way of making a living.

During this time, not only in his diocese but also in all Russia, people began refraining from receiving the Eucharist, except for four times a year (a practice that St. Tikhon would adamantly oppose later in his writings).

Nevertheless, he was determined to purge the Church of the increasing indifference that had seeped in. He began teaching and writing discourses for the priests and laity alike, putting forth strict regulations while never berating his flock. At the same time, St.

Tikhon became depressed, wondering why he could not be just a simple monk without the administrative responsibilities. His lapses into depression were something with which he struggled for a good part of his life. He also showed signs of some nervous disease, marked by giddiness and irritability. At times he would even faint during the Divine Liturgy.

In 1767, exhausted from the heavy demands of his position, he became quite ill and retired to a monastery. When his health showed little improvement, two years later, he went to the monastery of Zadonsk. As he was allowed to leave his administrative responsibilities behind him, his condition improved. In the monastic life, he seemed much more content and less irritable and melancholy. More importantly for our sake, it is here that he did the bulk of his writing.

On August 13, 1783, St. Tikhon died quietly before being able to receive the Holy Mysteries that he had requested when he sensed his earthly life was coming to a close. He was canonized in 1861.

St. Tikhon was no innovator or theologian, in the academic sense. His biographer, Nadejda Gorodetzky writes, "He claimed no originality; he wrote what belonged to the tradition. But he was the first to attempt to produce an accessible and integral presentation of Christian dogma in its application to the life of the individual and of society." As we shall see, the practical aspects of his writings are quite apparent. He was concerned about how Christians could live out their calling in a world drifting farther away from the Truth.

To discover how St. Tikhon developed his ideas on how to struggle against sin, it is beneficial to understand his concept of human nature. This saint's teachings are completely in agreement with the Holy Scriptures and the tradition of the Church. He writes, "Every Christian has two births, the old and fleshly, and the spiritual and new, and each is opposed to the other." Knowing the complacency that had settled into the parishioners, he adds, "For only those who have *crucified the flesh with its passions and desires* are Christians. What use is it to be called Christian, yet not truly be Christians? It is not the name of Christian that shows the true Christian, but the struggle against the flesh and against every sin. We must not permit the flesh everything it demands." Hence, for every baptized Christian, a struggle between the flesh and spirit must exist.

If we give the flesh everything it desires, then it will reign in our bodies; if, however, we deny its desires we begin gaining victory over our passions. It is not enough to say we are Christians, the saint teaches us; but we must struggle and fight the good fight so that we may become true Christians. In fact, his biographer tells us, "He saw Christian life as a valiant and continuous fight against self, against social evils and, deeper still, against the personal embodiment of evil." This spiritual warfare "should begin with self-knowledge, not as a matter of philosophical theory or of introspection, but as a practical necessity; in order to correct a deviation of the soul one must have a clear perception of what it is." This knowledge is impossible without knowing God and seeing ourselves in His light.

The first step we must take is to decide that we want to repent and to lead the Christian life. "Take no greater care than to correct your will and inward disposition. In this consists all the power of Christian piety." He goes on to write,

> All outwardness without inwardness is nothing. Whatever is not inside the heart does not exist in actual fact. Virtue is not true virtue when it is not within the heart. Therefore correct your heart and your will, and you shall be good and your outward deeds will be good, for the inward is the beginning of the outward. When evil is not in the heart, then it will not appear outwardly.

These words echo the teaching of our Savior. "But what comes out of the mouth proceeds from the heart, and this defiles a man. For out of the heart come evil thoughts, murder, adultery, fornication, theft, false witness, slander" (Matt. 15: 18-19); and "The good man out of the good treasure of his heart produces good, and the evil man out of his evil treasure produces evil; for out of the abundance of the heart his mouth speaks" (Luke 6:45).

This inner correction can take place only if we are able to acknowledge the sinfulness of our hearts. "It is not possible to correct yourself rightly if you do not recognize the evil hidden in your heart and the calamities that proceed from it. An unrecognized disease remains untreated." Of course, he realized that one could go too far the other direction and become discouraged at what was discovered in the heart. The heart is best revealed, according to the saint, during trials and temptations. "Temptations and trials show what is in the heart of a man." He encourages us by saying, "If, then, you fall into various temptations, O Christian, this all happens by God's permission for your great benefit, that you may thereby know what is hidden in your heart, and so knowing it you may correct yourself." He instructs us, "Do not become despondent in temptations, then, but give all the more thanks to God that He thus brings you to knowledge of yourself and wishes you to be corrected and be saved."

Before exploring some of St. Tikhon's suggestions for combating sin, we should look briefly at how the saint defines sin. He mentions several sins that are listed in the New Testament and are in accordance with Church tradition: pride, greed, fornication, gluttony, anger, lethargy, and envy. He also gives us six sins against the Holy Spirit:

> Despair which means having no hope in the mercy of God; presumption—too presumptuous reliance on his mercy; opposition to revealed truth, of the Holy Scriptures and of the dogmas of faith confirmed by the apostles and the holy fathers; envy the spiritual graces received from God by one's neighbor; obduracy in heresies and hardening in malice; negligence with regard to the salvation of the soul, till the end of one's life.

He also teaches us that four sins cry to God for vengeance: "deliberate murder; the vice of sodomy; embittering of the poor, of widows, and of orphans by offence and oppression; withholding or non-payment of wages to hired servants and workers."

He warns that indifference to such evil will harden the soul, making it unconscious of its estrangement from God. According to Nadejda Gorodetzky, for St.Tikhon, the most dangerous condition for a soul "is when it treats sin as a subject for joking."

How then are we to combat sin? He enumerates several ways to prepare ourselves for the battle. First, he teaches us to listen and obey the word of God. For Scripture "portrays sins and virtue, and leads us from sin and encourages us toward virtue." St. Tikhon encourages us to learn from the Gospels and imitate Christ. "Let the immaculate life of Christ be a mirror to your soul."

We must note that he does not separate the reading of Holy Scripture from the life of the Church. While he certainly does not discourage reading the Scriptures outside of Church service, he does emphasize, however, the importance of being attentive during the Divine Liturgy: "Listen diligently, reflect on what is read, and endeavor to put these words into practice. The word of God was not given to us in order that it should repose in writing on paper, but that we might use it spiritually, that we might be illumined, led into the way of truth and salvation, correct our manners, and live according to its rules in this world and do things well-pleasing to God." Thus, for St.Tikhon, the word of God is tied closely to participation in the Divine Liturgy: "The Church here on earth is not perfect, for she includes sinners as well as saints, but she gives to both opportunity for amendment, growth, perfection and sanctification."

Second, St. Tikhon teaches us that prayer is an important weapon in our fight against sin: "Our effort and struggle against sin is powerless without help from God. For this reason, we must make an effort to pray, that the Lord help us in this so important struggle." He also states, "Know, beloved, that a Christian without prayer is as a bird without wings and as a warrior without weapons."

Another way that St. Tikhon suggests for us to gain victory over sin is to remember the presence of God, a concept taught by the early Church Fathers. He writes, "God is present in every place, and He is with us wherever we may be. And we, anything we may do, we do before Him and His holy eyes." Again, he warns us, "Wherever you may go and wherever you may be, God is with you and knows and sees all your doings and hears your words. Then watch yourself everywhere." We must therefore be aware that each time we gossip about someone, become angry with another, have impure thoughts, or do any shameful deeds, that God is present and that we shall be held accountable for every deed and idle word spoken.

Avoiding all occasions that may lead to sin is still another way for us to overcome temptations: "Avoid occasions that lead to sin, such as banquets and feasting, and evil and useless conversations." For example, if we find that being around a certain person or group of people causes us to participate in gossip or idle conversations, we should avoid such persons at all cost, remembering that we must give an account for every idle word spoken (Matt. 12:36). Echoing the teaching from the epistle of St. James, St. Tikhon, writing about careless, gossiping Christians, states, "With one and the same mouth they slander their neighbor and whisper their prayers, sing to God and partake of the Body and Blood of Christ." His biographer writes, "He advocated prudence, avoidance of the company of slanderers, and prayer for others as a remedy against a haughty attitude towards them. But we must also pray about the guarding of the door of our lips." Avoiding gossip and idle talk is only an example of the saint's teaching on avoiding evil.

Applying his instruction to our own time, we may find it necessary to choose carefully what we watch or hear. Some, if not most, forms of contemporary entertainment serve to pollute our hearts and minds with evil and lies. Thus, when finding that certain activities are harmful to our souls, we must forgo them, so that the seeds of sin will not be sown in our hearts.

Listening to and obeying the word of God, along with prayer, the remembrance of God's presence, and the need to avoid occasions for sin are important for St. Tikhon's teachings on struggling against sin; they are not emphasized, however, as much as is the need to meditate upon our own death and final judgment: "Remember the last things: death, the Judgement of Christ, hell and the Kingdom of Heaven. These things deter sin." These sobering reflections are central to his instructions. He writes,

> Nothing so moves a sinner to repentance as eternity, and nothing is so useful to every Christian as remembrance and contemplation of eternity. Eternity restrains a man from sin, calms his passions, turns him from the world and all its vanity, makes his heart contrite, gives birth to tears of repentance, incites him to prayer, and works true sighing of the heart. Contemplation and remembrance of eternity can correct even the most depraved man.

For St. Tikhon, meditation on eternity embraces much of the Christian life, not the least of which is the overcoming of our sins.

The holy elder teaches us that the converse of remembrance—forgetfulness—is a major cause of sin. In the following statement, he touches on a "modern" problem that faces many contemporary Christians:

> It is amazing that Christians of the present age while hearing in the Holy Scriptures of eternity, are nevertheless so attached to the vanity of this world, and seek honors, glory, and riches in this world, build, add onto, and adorn their houses and other edifices, as though there were no eternity. Forgetfulness of eternity works this in them, and the enticement of the vanity of the eyes darkens their hearts.

Hence, according to St. Tikhon, forgetting eternity and all that it shall bring can lead to greed and materialism. If we want therefore to escape the cupidity of our age, we must contemplate eternity: our death, judgment, and eternal reward or punishment. Elsewhere he states, "Remember death often, and the judgment of Christ, eternal torment, and eternal life, and inevitably the world with all its lusts and enticements will become abhorrent to you." His writings reflect his awareness of death. For him, this remembrance not only strengthens us against sin, but it also sharpens our focus on an aspect of our existence that most choose to ignore.

> The longer we live, the more our life is diminished and our days are shortened and the more we approach death. And we are closer to death today than we were yesterday, this hour than we were last hour. Death walks invisibly behind every man and seizes him when he least suspects it.

Being aware of the unexpectancy of death should sober our lives so that we do not engage in sin. The saint warns us, "Keep in mind and remembrance that a man could die and perish in the very act of sin." He implores us therefore to meditate on the very hour of our repose.

> Let us inscribe that hour in our memory and let us be prepared. From that hour on a man will be either eternally blessed or eternally unhappy. Here the door to eternity is opened to each man, and he will go into either a happy or unhappy eternity. From that

point on a man begins to either
live eternally or die eternally.

Not only must we meditate on our death, but we must also contemplate our final judgment. St. Tikhon warns us: "Be horrified to sin and commit iniquity. God Himself is coming to judge you, He is coming with might and great glory." He paints a vivid picture of that great, terrible day:

> At a human trial only outward deeds are judged. At that judgment [before God], secret thoughts as well. At a human trial only evil deeds are judged. At that judgment, also every idle word. . .. If we shall give account for every idle word, what shall those people expect who defile soul and body with impurity, who pour out widows' and orphans' tears, who rob and steal others' goods, who cut and strike at their neighbors with their tongue as with a sword, who dissemble and deceive people.

It is no wonder that with such meditations, one would have an increased desire to avoid sin. Yet it would be a mistake to believe that he was pessimistic or even negative. His desire was not to have people live in constant fear; what he wanted to produce in himself and others was sobriety. He knew the importance of living a life of holiness and discipline and he knew that conscious awareness of death and judgment was a means to those ends. In fact, the judgment was an event for which we should be thankful. He writes,

> Through the promise of good things God calls us to Himself and to eternal salvation, but through the threat of punishment He incites, compels, and convinces. He threatens sinners for the reason that he does not wish to destroy them. He manifests His wrath for this reason, that out of fear of it we should correct ourselves and escape eternal punishment. For the threat of punishment moves us more toward repentance than the promise of good things....

He also believed that meditating on the joy set before us was of great help to our souls. He taught that those who fear death should recall

> the guiltless passion of Christ; the resurrection of our bodies; the angels who carry our souls to God; the beginning of a new and better life, where we shall see God, where there will be the

amiable society of the Queen of Heaven and of the saints; where we shall become free from this world into which we were born with a cry—for a devout soul feels always like a stranger till it reaches its homeland of heaven. There will it rest from strife and labor—and it will be in eternal rest.

Accordingly, in our struggle with sin, we should meditate on the possibility of either eternal punishment or eternal joy. Both have their place in our contemplation. He suggests that we practice such meditation at night, just before sleeping.

All the tools of the Christian life are important in our struggle with sin, such as prayer, obedience to the Scriptures, and attentiveness during the Divine Liturgy. St. Tikhon's teachings, as we have seen, emphasize above all the need for meditation. He writes,

> Meditate more often, O Christian, on eternity, that you may better escape sin. One cannot think of eternity without sighing and fear. Meditation upon eternity makes weeping and tears sweet, it lightens every toil, it teaches us to accept with thanksgiving any temporal

punishment, sorrow, offence, dishonor, banishment and death itself; it prevents us from falling into the snare of lawlessness. He who thinks of eternity will seek the word of God and instruction to salvation more than he seeks his daily food.

It is clear that, for him, meditation on eternity—and all of its possibilities—was central not only to our struggle against sin, but to all of the Christian life.

The holy elder knew that despite all of our struggles, we would at times succumb to sin. He urges us to remember the mercy of God: "There is more mercy in God than sins in us, provided we have sincere repentance; acknowledge, confess your sin at once, whatever it happens to be." We must therefore repent immediately and confess our sin.

Finally, St. Tikhon offers us a good summary of his vast teachings on our struggle against sin. He states,

Attend to the things that can free you from sin: the omnipresence of God; prayer; communion; the suffering of

Christ; our ignorance as to the hour of our death; eternal pain; sin in itself as a deed of the devil; sorrow and grief for offending our Father. If nothing else avails to stop you, abstain from sin if only for fear of remorse in your conscience. And pray for the gifts of the Spirit.

No better summary can be given.

Pray for us, St. Tikhon, that through the practice of spiritual warfare, we may be strengthened in our struggle against sin.

Bibliography

Gorodetzky, Nadejda. *Saint Tikhon of Zadonsk: Inspirer of Dostoevsky.* Crestwood, NY: St. Vladimir's Seminary Press, 1976.

Tikhon of Zadonsk. *Journey to Heaven: Counsels on the Particular Duties of Every Christian.* Translated by Fr. George D. Lardas. Jordanville, NY: Holy Trinity Monastery, Printshop of St. Job of Pochaev, 1991.

Made in the USA
Columbia, SC
04 April 2019